DIGITAL MOVIEMAKING 3

SCOTT BILLUPS

MICHAEL WIESE PRODUCTIONS

Published by Michael Wiese Productions

3940 Laurel Canyon Blvd. – Suite 1111

Studio City, CA 91604

(818) 379-8799, (818) 986-3408 (FAX).

mw@mwp.com

www.mwp.com

Cover design by MWP

Printed by McNaughton & Gunn

Printed on Recycled stock

Manufactured in the United States of America

Copyright 2007 Scott Billups

Library of Congress Cataloging-in-Publication Data

Billups, Scott.

 Digital moviemaking 3.0 / Scott Billups.

     p. cm.

 ISBN 978-1-932907-37-7

 1. Digital cinematography. I. Title.

 TR860.B463 2008

 778.5'3--dc22

                    2007034950

"Master digital filmmaker Scott Billups covers the essentials and shares critical tips and techniques that only an industry insider could know. His conversational style and first-hand knowledge make this book a great read for anyone serious about creating films with digital tools. This is not a dry, technical tome; it comes to life with Billup's authenticity, personal perspective, and vast experience."

— Lynda Weinman, founder, *lynda.com*

"This book is required reading for any filmmaker who wants to be on the cutting edge of the digital revolution. Scott Billups is the first guy I turn to for the latest in what's going on in digital moviemaking. How great that this new info is in book form! This is the bible for all digital filmmakers, packed with valuable information for the first-time filmmaker as well as for the most sophisticated of the digerati."

— Randal Kleiser, director (*Grease, The Blue Lagoon, Big Top Pee-wee*)

"This book details everything you need to know about digital moviemaking, explaining it all in a clear and concise way. Buy a copy before you start filming: you'll be glad you did."

— Matthew Terry, *www.hollywoodlitsales.com*

"This is the perfect book for those who are just beginning their venture into the world of digital microcinema filmmaking. It is easy to understand, very enjoyable to read, and will be a valuable asset in learning how to bring your stories to life on screen."

— Kari Ann Morgan, assistant editor, *Microfilmmaker Magazine*

"If you're serious about making movies, Scott Billups' *Digital Moviemaking 3.0* is bound to please. It covers an amazing amount of fertile ground in less than 250 pages. WARNING: this is not a how-to for hobbyists, but a kick-in-the-pants approach to HDV that encourages 'integrity' and vision in the filmmaking process. In the dangerous world of DV, everyone can use a weapon, and this might just be it."

— Derek Pell, editor-in-chief, *DingBat Magazine*

"Screenwriters and other filmmakers need to be more entrepreneurial than ever to move their career to the next level. For those who grab hold of that challenge and set out to make a film to show what they can do, there has not been a more practical guide than *Digital Moviemaking 3.0* to turn a script into a digital film. With Scott Billups' book in your back pocket, you'll have the professional know-how to make a film that stands out."

— Charles B. Slocum, Assistant Executive Director, Writers Guild of America, West

"Scott Billups is one of the pioneers who macheted a path through the wilderness of digital filmmaking. There is no better guide for the journey."

— Paula Parisi, Vice President & Executive Editor, *The Hollywood Reporter*

"If you are entering into the new world of digital filmmaking and you want to know everything about everything, read this book by Scott Billups. You'll be sorry if you don't."

— David Lynch, director

"If Bukowski or Henry Miller knew how to fix anything at all — even a toaster — and tried to write about it, they would've sounded like Scott Billups, who takes technology out of protected pockets and puts it between his legs where all good art and life resides."

— Erika Lopez, author, screenwriter

In Memory of
Marlon Brando

A good friend for more than half my life, Marlon was family.

"The seismic wave of change is collapsing on each of us. Unless we understand something of its nature, we will be swept away into a third intellectual world. Scott's book has served as guide and mentor for me and has been a critical assist in helping me to understand the world of digital technology. For those who are bewildered and stumbling in their efforts to comprehend this new world of communication technology, this is the definitive manual."

— Marlon Brando

TABLE OF CONTENTS

CHAPTER 6. DIGITAL CINEMATOGRAPHY 68

CHAPTER 7. CAST 'N' CREW

CHAPTER 8. DIGITAL CRAFTSMANSHIP

CHAPTER 9. HACKS

CHAPTER 1

PIXELMONGER MANIFESTO

This is not another introductory, "how-to-make-a-movie" book. It is not intended to take someone who just got their first camcorder and a personal computer and walk them through the production process.

This book is geared to professional-minded people who have hopefully had prior experience in some aspect of production and who understand the fundamental difference between a hobby and a career. It is about how to be successful at making movies. Not the kind of movies that you have to bribe your friends to watch, but the kind of movies that 14-year-old boys, on their first date with the girl next door, line up for on a Saturday night.

HDV moviemaking is not about introducing content into the conventional motion picture distribution stream. It never was. It never will be. It is about an affordable, entry-level acquisition and post-production environment that gives people an opportunity to experiment and demonstrate their abilities. It is about people going out and self-starting a project, involving others who might or might not find that they have a flair or interest in making movies.

You get something good down on HDV and show it around: festivals, private screenings, DVD, podcasts, the internet, whatever. If someone likes it, they might give you a crack at a commercial project that will then be shot on a professional format like film, HD or 2K..

There have been a handful of projects shot on HDV and miniDV that have gained a modicum of success, but even the few established industry luminaries who have used them cinematically seem to regret their "artistic" choices. Just because you can, doesn't mean you should.

The aesthetics of integrity that once endowed emerging moviemakers has been corrupted by snake-oil salesmen who promise to throw open the gates of Hollywood to anyone who buys their latest product — hardware, software, cameras, accessories — as though without the newest, latest, fastest your chances of success are something less.

My goal is to kick your professionalism, your toolset and your image quality up a notch so that you can compete in the real world of cinema. After you've learned the methodology and made your mistakes, and it finally comes time for you to make your cinematic entree, the only formats you should consider using are Pro-HD or film.

There are no simple solutions, secret tricks, instant remedies or gizmos that will turn you into a moviemaker. The odds are against you for a number of reasons. Some we can do something about, some we can't. My only promise to you is that by the time you've finished this book, your odds of success will have improved.

CLICHÉS THAT KILL

The word passion gets thrown around a lot in this industry. *"You've got to have a real passion for filmmaking,"* they'll tell you. It is an easy phrase to use and looks real good in print, but the rancid alleyways of Hollywood Boulevard are full of kids who came to this town with a belly full of passion. Passion blinds you; it is only your unyielding death grip on reality that will guarantee any measure of success in this business.

There are other gratuitous clichés that get thrown around like *"have faith in your abilities."* As though with faith alone you can surmount all obstacles. *"Follow your dream"* is perhaps the most hideous cliché of all because it panders to people who simply don't have any other options. There is no cosmic external force that will turn a bad script into gold or make the clock move slower so you can catch up with your production schedule. There are no new stories to tell, no angles to exploit, no trends to follow.

The path through Hollywood was worn smooth long ago by people wearing shoes much bigger than yours or mine. Craft is important in making a quality movie, but without a firm grasp of the realities of the market and industry, you're just another slab of meat spread out on the deli tray.

Jeff Dowd is a prominent and outspoken Hollywood producer who drags his long, unbroken string of successful movies around like toilet paper stuck to the bottom of his shoe. Here is a man hard to impress. Perhaps it is his unyielding devotion to the fundamentals that has allowed such a gregarious character to flourish in Hollywood. *"Last year in the United States alone there were thousands of movies shot on DV,"* he told those in attendance at a recent IFP seminar. *"They all sucked!"*

With so much easy access and hype, independent moviemaking has festered into a vast amalgam of self-indulgent mediocrity. The "Indie look" has become more of a marketing strategy than alternative methodology. The irresistible lure of instant "hip" has caused a growing number of directors who should know better, to prove they don't.

I attended the Cannes Film Festival orientation a while back and it was quite an eye opener. Of the thousands of applicants vying for the four American spaces in the festival, there were only a dozen of us sitting there. That's thousands of lives that were put on hold, houses mortgaged, life savings drained, marriages strained, and I'll bet every one of them thought they were a shoo-in for the *Palme d'Or.*

The assault of thousands of semi-literate people with their half-baked, get-rich-quick schemes has taken its toll on the motion picture industry. A few well-connected kids with famous parents might make a ripple here or there, but the odds are stacked against you and they are simply overwhelming.

To make a living as a moviemaker in the digital age, you need to have good communication skills, a good eye, and an above-average understanding of the desktop production environment. You also need to understand what motivates and engages people, and how to push their buttons.

> Passion blinds you; it is only your unyielding death grip on reality that will guarantee any measure of success in this business.

Next, you need balls of steel (or ovaries as the case may be), and skin as thick as old shoe leather. A strong persistence of vision that borders on "jackass stubborn" will also serve you well as you continually forge past those who feel the urgent need to add their dos centavos to your little gem of a project.

Above all, you'll need an inspired point of view as well as the will and determination to get your project made. Even if you possess all of the previously mentioned traits, without consummate people skills you've only got another pathetic side-show looking to hitch a ride with the grandest circus of them all.

To quote the always acerbic Dennis Miller, *"From Balinese shadow plays to bullfighters in Madrid to the porn studios of the San Fernando Valley ... the only human desire more universal than the urge to put on a show is the urge to get paid for it."*

So welcome to the freak show, my friend. I hope you're wearing your bulletproof, Eddie Bauer, safari-slash-director's jacket, because there's nothing that this industry loves more than a well-dressed corpse.

CHAPTER 2

CONTEXT

Until you have actually participated in the motion picture manufacturing process, the vast majority of your information with regard to
production comes from books, articles and word-of-mouth. There's
really nothing wrong with this as long as you keep everything in
context.

Context is the mental process of making connections based on
personal experience and available facts within the capacity of your
intelligence.

Easily our most essential learning tool, context is critical in judging
our actions within society. Without a good grasp of context you are at
the mercy of the media and can easily live your entire life from within
the illusions that are marketed at you.

With all due respect: The goal of this book is to break through the
patina of highly polished bullshit that reflects off of the fart bubbles of
facts that drift through this industry.

To understand how to succeed in the motion picture industry, or
in life for that matter, we must grasp the subtle difference between
DATA, INFORMATION and KNOWLEDGE. Together they can
help you filter all the clutter and become your compass headings
through life.

Data generally exists as a compilation of proven facts that have been
generated by testing or observation. It exists in isolation until there
is context. This is perhaps why all the successful moviemakers test
everything, all the time.

The tests in this book have not been transposed from some other
work or passed by word of mouth, or gleaned from a press release. I
am however, not above poaching off of tests that my friends do.

My information may not come from the fanciest or most spectacular tests you've ever seen, but they all provided relevant data that
enhanced my knowledge and allowed me to make informed decisions
and recommendations.

An example of one of my tests can be seen at: *http://www.cinematography.net/hdcamtests/pixelmonger.htm*

That test was done to compare the HD-SDI signal from a Thompson Viper camera to the HD-SDI signal of a Canon XLH-1. Although no one had ever actually done a side-by-side comparison of those two cameras before, there were hundreds, if not thousands, of opinions flying around passing as fact.

While not to be considered a definitive test between two widly differeing cameras, this side-by-side comparison of the Thomson Viper and the Canon XLH1 was considered to have made a very compelling argument for direct-to-disk aqusition.

Was this the definitive test of two vastly different cameras? No way. The context of the test, although conducted in a well-documented environment that was attended by widely respected industry professionals, was relatively superficial in its scope. I got the DATA that I needed, shared it as INFORMATION on the most reputable international forum for cinematography that I know of (CML), and went on to other things.

The results of that test were screened for various industry associations and individuals and I would assume that everyone, within the CONTEXT of their SITUATION became more KNOWLEDGEABLE.

There are billions of dollars spent each year in an attempt to alter the context of your information and rearrange your priorities. Advertising is data that has been framed with non-contextual information, PR is data that is framed by enhanced information, and hype is data that is framed by false information.

The only hope you have of breaking through the mythos is to develop your sense of context.

An average person, living in a modern country, is bombarded with more than five thousand media messages a day. Every single one of them wants to mess with your sense of context. Every single one of them wants you to believe that you'll get better results, or be more successful, or make more money, or smell fresher if you use their product or service.

Ask yourself, where did the information come from? What is that person's experience? What is their motive? Are they trying to sell you something? Are they looking for company in their own misery? Where is the profit and who gets it?

I've received thousands of emails from readers of my books and articles. The beginning of every day, whether on set, on a plane or pick'n my nose (yes, I can type with one hand), starts by answering the email that makes it through my 50-word limit filter.

In the eight years since the first edition of *Digital Moviemaking* hit the shelves, there hasn't been a legitimate question that I haven't taken a try at answering.

Much of the email is from people who have read, and re-read, both the first and second editions of this book numerous times. While this is enormously flattering, it was obvious that I needed to make things easier to understand the first time. I intend to do that by spending a bit more time establishing context.

> An average person, living in a modern country, is bombarded with more than five thousand media messages a day.

Since the last edition of this book hit the shelves I've shot seven motion pictures, five of them digitally. Except for two that were studio projects, all were featured at major festivals like Sundance/Slamdance, Toronto and the HBO Comedy festival in Aspen. All have sold, gone into distribution, and made money.

In that same time period I've also written, directed, done visual effects and/or produced more than a dozen award-winning shows for Discovery Channel, History Channel and HBO, and worked on both of this year's non-fiction, prime-time Emmy winners. I've also managed to take a concept through scripting all the way to the pilot stage for a major network sale.

Yes, business is very good for Scotty these days, but the reason that I even bring it up is to establish the context of this book. My experience is the source of the facts from which I draw my conclusions. My data comes from copious testing, my information comes from applying that to my personal experience, and my knowledge comes from a rather successful career in an ever-changing industry.

If this book seems a bit braggadocios at times, I apologize. There is a fine line between example and blatant self-aggrandizement. I endeavor to do my best to maintain an arc of illustrative allegory and analysis, but truth is, you just can't make it in this business without a little P. T. Barnum in your soul.

In the process of laying out the digital landscape for working industry professionals, I am addressing a few gaping holes in the previous versions of this book. The flip side is that I've been taking notes: what works, what doesn't. What people like, what they don't. Some of the same questions keep popping up time and again, and with new technologies come new questions.

That said, I am de-tech-ifying this edition. A lot of the stuff that was important to know a few years ago, just isn't as important now that the market has stabilized and digital has become ubiquitous.

> Truth is, you just can't make it in this business without a little P. T. Barnum in your soul.

The whole *Printing to Film* chapter has been retired since none of the major film festivals require it any more. If your digital movie does get picked up, the distributor will gladly pay the costs involved with printing to film.

The lengthy comparisons between analog and digital systems have been pulled since they seem irrelevant now that high-quality digital acquisition is so affordable.

Here, in this third book in the *Digital Moviemaking* series, I'm pretty much rebuilding it all from the ground up. Except for a few bits that everyone seems to like, the industry has change so dramatically that you're holding an entirely different animal. Hopefully this will all be useful to you as I end this chapter with my favorite explanation of context.

SIX MEN OF INDOSTAN

It was six men of Indostan

To learning much inclined,

Who went to see the Elephant

(Though all of them were blind),

That each by observation

Might satisfy his mind

The First approached the Elephant,
And happening to fall
Against his broad and sturdy side,
At once began to bawl:
"God bless me! but the Elephant
Is very like a wall!"

The Second, feeling of the tusk,
Cried, "Ho! what have we here
So very round and smooth and sharp?
To me 'tis mighty clear
This wonder of an Elephant
Is very like a spear!"

The Third approached the animal,
And happening to take
The squirming trunk within his hands,
Thus boldly up and spake:
"I see," quoth he, "the Elephant
Is very like a snake!"

The Fourth reached out an eager hand,
And felt about the knee.
"What most this wondrous beast is like
Is mighty plain," quoth he;
"'Tis clear enough the Elephant
Is very like a tree!"

The Fifth, who chanced to touch the ear,
Said: "E'en the blindest man
Can tell what this resembles most;
Deny the fact who can
This marvel of an Elephant
Is very like a fan!"

The Sixth no sooner had begun
About the beast to grope,
Than, seizing on the swinging tail
That fell within his scope,
"I see," quoth he, "the Elephant
Is very like a rope!"

And so these men of Indostan
Disputed loud and long,
Each in his own opinion
Exceeding stiff and strong,
Though each was partly in the right,
And all were in the wrong!
Moral:
So oft in theologic wars,
The disputants, I ween,
Rail on in utter ignorance
Of what each other mean,
And prate about an Elephant
Not one of them has seen!

- John Godfrey Saxe

CHAPTER 3

MOORE'S LAW

*A calculator on the ENIAC is equipped with 19,000
vacuum tubes and weighs 30 tons, computers in the
future may have only 1,000 vacuum tubes and perhaps
only weigh 1.5 tons.*
- *Popular Mechanics*, March 1949.

Back in 1962, Intel co-founder Gordon Moore was sitting around with a few of his "pocket protector" buds, enjoying a few drinks. Well, ol' Gordon made a prediction and it must'a sounded cool, because one of his egghead buddies wrote it down on a cocktail napkin: *"The logic density of silicon integrated circuits should follow the curve (bits per square inch) = 2n(t-1962) where t is time in years."*

A few years pass by, Gordon's bud is cleaning out his desk and finds that old cocktail napkin that says curvy thing = 2 pointy thing, t-1962. Being a geek, he pulls a pen out of his pocket protector, does a few quick calculations of his own. Gord-o's little equation was bang on.

Translated into English, Moore's little hypothesis states that computing power, at any given price point, doubles every 18 months, while cost and size are reduced by half.

This became known as Moore's Law, and it holds true for everything from the speed and capacity of RAM and hard drives to the peripherals that we use to sample and gather data. Since HD cameras are technically computer peripherals, they are subject to Moore's Law along with all the other digital bits.

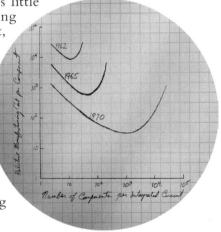

Perhaps Moore's Law was little more than a casual observation over a few too many cocktails, but its performance quite literally speaks for itself. It is not just a pair of intersecting vectors, but rather a three-dimensional matrix that is so accurate that you would be hard pressed to find a successful technology manufacturer that does not adhere to it religiously.

Allow me to illustrate this point with my own experience.

Back in 1989 I created what is widely considered to be the first fully digital show. The goal was to shoot and edit a show entirely on the hard disk of a computer, then take the computer to the television station and broadcast it directly from the hard disk.

It was called *A Day in the Life of Melrose Ave*, and the entire show was created within the digital domain, never touching tape.

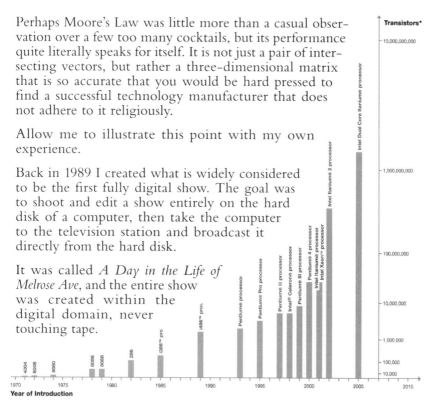

Attempting that today is no big thing, a FireWire drive and a laptop, but this was well before the era of affordable gigabyte drives.

The show was fun but somewhat anti-climatic domestically because hardly anyone realized what had just been done. There was no reference or context, and as we all know, technology without context is irrelevant.

The Japanese, however, had their own context. Within two weeks of the show's airing, I found myself sitting in the Sony headquarters in Shinagawa, Japan. They unveiled an endless procession of production environments that give a razor-sharp oracle of what was around our technological corner.

Keep in mind that I had been writing about film and video production technology for five of the leading industry magazines for quite a while. If anyone should have a clue about this stuff it should be me.

What I saw completely blew my mind. How could I have been so blind to what was in the pipes? It became apparent that what we perceive as the bleeding edge of technology, even those of us writing about it, is only a carefully orchestrated ballet of illusion.

Once back from Japan, the digital camera concept became an obsession, every iteration getting smaller, with greater capacity and more resolution. The first truly luggable (as opposed to portable) camera system came off the benches in mid-1992.

It took the RGB signal directly off of the imaging chips and recorded it in compressed 8bit; 4:1:1 to the hard drive using a prototype Video Explorer videographic board custom made by my good friend, and nerd savant, Brett Bilbrey (now at Apple).

Since we were going for quality as opposed to quantity, the drive could only hold 23 seconds of video at a time. Still, we used it on several jobs and kept on moving.

OK, it was incredibly dorky looking, but it worked. Who would believe that in less than just a few years even better resolution would be available in a pocket-sized form-factor?

Several years later I got a call from someone at the Academy of Television Arts & Sciences, asking if I knew that Avid was campaigning for an Emmy. It seems they were claiming that they had developed the digital camcorder.

The author with the first digital camcorder.

They'd taken the same camera head (now called the HL-76), updated the same basic design and called it the CamCutter. I reminded them that there was a very nice article in the August '93 issue of their own *Emmy Magazine*, with a lovely picture of me standing there holding my homemade digital camcorder that predated the Avid claim by more than two years. Never really heard much about it after that.

Back in 1989, when we shot that little "all-digital" show, we used a new hard drive that could record data at an unbelievable 6Mb/sec. My friends all thought that I had lost my mind. After all, what could anyone possibly need with a gigabyte of storage?

Plug that into Moore's law and we get a relative point of reference. At $5,000 it was very expensive; at 24 pounds, it was very heavy; and while a GB was considered quite large in 1989, by contemporary standards it is very small. Add to that a transfer speed of 6Mb/sec and you get a system that is quite literally pathetic by today's standards.

Flash forward 18 years and you can see the effect of Moore's Law everywhere. Price and size have diminished greatly while performance and capacity have increased.

Today nearly everyone has a phone that not only has enormous storage and computational power but also takes pictures and records movies.

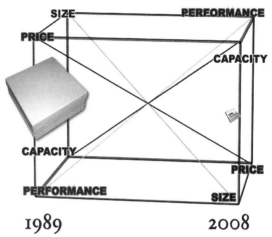

1989   2008

Plug that into Moore's Law and you'll see why it is so important to develop a sound production methodology regardless of the price or size of your format.

In another five or ten years, the only thing that will separate moviemakers from the guy with a new phone is craft and methodology.

If you want to know where something digital is going, look at where it was five or ten years ago, look at where it is now and then plot out the price, size, capacity and performance vectors.

For illustration, if the automobile industry performed at the same level, today's Mercedes sedan, which in 1972 cost around $10K, would cost 12 cents, get 10,000 MPG and travel near the speed of light.

With the industry-wide acceptance of digital, the motion picture indstry has plugged into that formula. As fast as things are changing now, the next ten years should be quite amazing.

Now that Moore's Law has been running amok for nearly 40 years, I'm starting to notice a strange little phenomenon that we can call "Scotty's Observation" for lack of a better name. The one factor that is missing from Moore's law is ergonomics.

iTele-Phoneto-Cam?

At some point things get so small that they become awkward and the "size" vector of Moore's Law ceases to be germane. ~ Billups '07

A good example is Apple's video iPod, released in 2006. Technically, it was well aligned with all of Moore's vectors, but the screen was just too small for comfortable viewing.

Many people who actually needed and used a portable media player switched to the larger screens of either the PSP or the Creative Zen. But then there is Steve Jobs; a man who obviously keeps his eye on Moore's vectors.

The iPhone not only put the iPod line back on track, but it established a new vector cross-over point for communications, information and entertainment.

Moore's vectors indicate that in just a few years the iPhone will be recording 1080 Progressive HD via its built-in camera. It will have a very nice micro version of FinalCut that will allow you to edit your shots on the run. By looking at the vectors of cellular communication and non-terrestrial transmission we can count on being able to squirt each other HD in real-time, regardless of proximity.

VECTOR SCHMECTOR

How accurate is Moore's Law? For those of you who might have the first edition of this book (circa 1999) lying around, I invite you to turn to page 216. For those of you who are just joining us, I'll cut-and-paste the page for you here.

One of the most common remarks with respect to that version of the book was with respect to *"outlandish"* and *"unfounded"* visions of the future that it proposed. It is with moderate humility that I mention that they've all appeared on schedule.

~~~ P#216 - DM first edition circa 1999 ~~~

Micro movie venues are about to cascade down from the technological heaven. They'll eventually be integrated into just about everything you can imagine.

A brisk walk up the Ginza will take you past hundreds of people walking to work, shopping or just leaning up against a building. In their hands are a wide assortment of micro-miniaturized portable venues.

Phones playing streaming video in diminutive screens, ultra-tiny LCD panels playing movies from postage stamp–sized RAM cards.

The chasm between the theatre screen and the handheld device is a big one. Each environment requires certain production considerations, but neither can become exclusive of the other.

Kind of interesting really, how even if you're shooting a multi-million dollar movie, the original shot is seen on a tiny screen within the camera's viewfinder.

Due to its close proximity to the observer the relative viewing size of this PCMCIA, video card exceeds the average home television's perceived size.

Micro-screens, head-mounted displays and corneal refracting devices are all coming soon to a Circuit City near you. In a way, the coming trend of handhelds is perhaps the most intimate and personal venue yet. Until the day when the first cyber-squatter jacks in to re-runs of I Love Lucy, we're on a one-way, no-holds-barred, smack-down battle for human attention.

Compression is the key to this digital future, whether used for down-linking a data stream for theatrical release or bouncing some homespun content off of a fan's cornea halfway around the world. Where it all ends up is a matter of conjecture, but I can promise you that it will be a most exhilarating ride.

~~~

CHAPTER 4

HD IS LIKE A BOX OF CRAYONS

Or: Everything you need to know about digital acquisition, you learned in kindergarten

With profound apologies to Robert Zimeckis and Tom Hanks, let's imagine that HD is like a box of crayons.

DATA RATE is the size of your box,

LATITUDE is the number of gray crayons between white and black,

COLOR SPACE is the number of crayons in your box and

SAMPLE RATE is the size of the actual crayons.

A digital moviemaker needs to have a basic understanding of the technologies involved in the manufacturing process.

Once you understand these four things, you will be able to make relatively intelligent format choices for the rest of your career.

DATA RATE

The amount of information that can be transmitted in a given period of time is called data rate or bandwidth.

Much like the top speed of a car can give you some quantitative understanding of its performance, a camera system's Data Rate can give you an idea of its potential performance. In both examples there are numerous qualitative issues to be considered as well.

Just because a camera can generate a lot of data, doesn't necessarily mean that it will give you the best image. Inversely, more and more low data rate cameras are producing better-looking images than ever before.

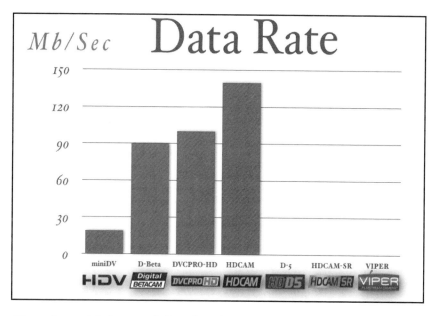

Plotted out this is essentially what the three most popular professional digital formats look like when compared to HDV. At a rather anemic 20Mb/sec, the data rate of HDV falls quite short of even the most popular standard definition format, DigiBeta.

The 90Mb/sec signal from a well-tuned DigiBeta not only holds up well to the qualitative impact of post-production, but has enough bulk to handle substantial color correction and even does quite well when up-converted and printed to film.

A short step up from DigiBeta is Panasonic's DVCPRO-HD. At 100Mb/sec it is considered to be the true start of HD.

Although the DVCPRO-HD line ranges from the $3,000 HVX series up to the $100,000+ VariCam series, many ads and owners of the HVX would like you to believe that they are the same: they aren't. There simply is no free lunch on the vectors of Moore's Law.

The quality of the VariCam is far superior on a number of different fronts. I have used them both, shot them side-by-side and compared them on many levels.

Anyone who says that the image from a $3,000 dollar camera is comparable to that of a camera costing 40 times as much is either delusional or lying to your face.

Having shot nearly 100 projects on the SONY F-900 series, I have begrudgingly become a fan of the HDCAM tape format. It is, in my opinion, the minimum requirement for major, theatrical distribution.

Sean Fairburn fires up the trusty F-900

It takes a lot of work to make the 3:1:1 HDCAM screen-worthy and is not something that you want to attempt straight out of the box.

You can blow up images from far less expensive cameras, but in the end, the audience can tell. Look at Robert Rodriguez's *Once Upon a Time in Mexico* to see how good the F-900 series can look.

I might even offer up a few of my own motion pictures since the same operator (Sean Fairburn) shot for both of us.

Barely more than a hot-rodded DigiBeta, the F-900 came to the end of its long and rather impressive life cycle several years ago according to Moore's Law.

The fact that there are so many of them in daily use indicates factors outside Moore's unyielding vectors.

Arguably, the 144Mb/sec signal is not the last word in quality, but as tape acquisition goes, the HDCAM series has proven itself to be a tireless workhorse.

The deep dark secret of most professional format cameras is that the imager (camera head) creates a much higher quality signal than the onboard video tape can record.

Not just a little better either: In numerous instances the HD-SDI image off of the chips is ten times the data rate of the onboard tape system or more.

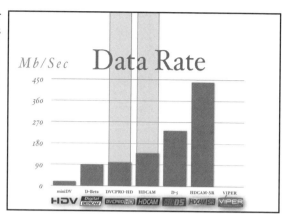

Even the highest data rate tape formats, such as D-5 at 235Mb/sec and Sony's HDCAM-SR at 440Mb/sec, can't compare with the native image from conventional camera heads. They are, however, very popular alternatives for people looking to get a better image from existing gear.

Recording the camera's HD-SDI signal to a higher data rate system is the fastest and easiest way to upgrade the inherent quality of your image.

The Panasonic D5 AJ-HD3700 has been the machine of choice for studio HD recording for quite a few years. It records 16:9 aspect ratio at full bandwidth, 10-bit component with a 180MHz sampling rate and 960 lines of resolution switchable to 1920x1080 at 24 or 30 fps at 2:1 on-the-fly compression.

Panasonic D-5

It has eight-channel PCM audio at 20 bits and does all flavors of HD at 10-bit quality with 4:2:2 color and mild bit rate reduction.

It is a great machine but unfortunately weighs slightly more than John Madden and is far less portable. A D5 tape, storing full-aspect 16x9 at 10-bit and 1,900 lines of resolution will give you around 40 minutes for slightly under $300 per cassette.

The last few years have seen a drastic erosion of the well-established D5 market segment by the Sony SRW. Arguably the end of the road for tape, the SRW records in full 4:4:4 color space via the dual link HD-SDI video I/O with 12 ch. audio at 24bits.

I've used both the Panasonic D-5 and the Sony SRW-1 extensively and never lost a pixel from either.

Sony SRW-1

One of the outstanding features of both systems is the ease with which they integrate into the desktop production environment.

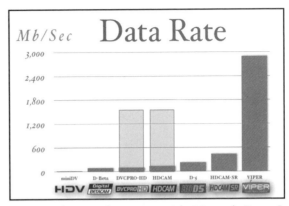

The problems inherent in tape-based acquisition are insurmountable. Tape is a retro-mechanical metaphor that is trying its best to keep up with Moore's Law. It is a losing proposition. In its defense, tape-based work flows fit much easier into conventional post metaphors than disk-based work flows.

Nearly every post house has aisles of racks that are full of the rapidly depreciating remnants of the mechanical age. They desperately need to amortize their investments. They need you to use tape. The true magnitude of this discontinuity is only revealed when you introduce the first widely used production camera that isn't hobbled by the finite limitations of tape.

Unhindered by the need to develop a system that could be integrated into a pre-existing, tape-based inventory, Thomson created the Viper. Because of its rugged dependability and raw acquisition mode, it instantly became the preeminent gold standard in ultra-high definition acquisition.

The author shoots some pirates with a Viper.

I've shot with the Viper quite a bit, and have used a wide range of gear to record as much of its freaking huge data rate of 1.4Gb/sec in 4:2:2 mode and 2.8Gb/sec in dual HD-SDI mode as I could.

As a point of reference, it would take the signal from 150 HDV camcorders, all recording simultaneously, to approximate the signal quality of one Viper running in FilmStream mode.

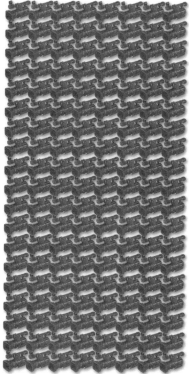

But wait: Didn't I just read somewhere that HDV was a professional cinema format?

After the Viper started becoming the darling of the high-end filmmakers, the other manufacturers were quick to jump on the data-rate bandwagon.

Viper

Sony ripped the cassette recorder off of their trusty F-900, upgraded the chip-set and introduced the F-950, which was then upgraded to the F23. It does a lightly compressed 4:4:4 and, having used them both rather extensively and consider the F23 to be the only competition that the Viper has in this specific market niche

The Panavision Genesis inte-

Sony f23

grated the Sony SRW-1 VTR into its camera design and introduced the first camera / recorder combo that could record dual-link 4:4:4 HD-SDI. When combined with a mild compression it put the camcorder back in the race.

Arri, long known for their fine film cameras, unveiled their D20 digital camera. It generates a whopping 10Gb/sec. through its innovative data buss and has incorporated many of the film-like features that old-school cinematographers like. Image quality aside, the optical viewfinder is easily the favorite attribute of this technological masterpiece.

Genesis

Arri D20

And then there is DALSA. One of the industry's leading chip manufacturers entered the high-stakes digital poker game with a 4046x2048 imager that captures 4:4:4, RGB at 4K resolution and 16 bits per channel. That's over 8 megapaixels, folks.

Heavy enough to give even the burliest gaffers hernias and only slightly smaller than a MiniCooper, the Dalsa can choke the heartiest of systems with a data rate nearly twice that of a Viper.

Dalsa Origin

I recently joined my good friend Dave Stump in an official ASC test of the new Olympus 4K camera. Its four Bayered CCDs put out a 3890x2160 signal via the Quad HD-SDI taps. That's four HD-SDI taps, each pumping out about 1.4Gb/sec.

We had a prototype 4K monitor with us and in one of the shots we did, we held the monitor up to the real scene and we all agreed that we liked the on-screen image better. Yes, we were all geeks.

The Olympus 4K camera feeding a 4K monitor.

We should all start getting comfortable with disk acquisition systems since the Sony SRW is technically the end of the road for tape.

RAM is technically a much better approach but broadbased integration is still a few years off on Moore's vectors.

Having shot with the RAM-based Panasonic HPX3000, it is easy to see what is around the collective corner for us all.

Although data rate can sometimes seem like a bad thing, the more you have, the bigger your box of crayons with which to paint your scenes.

Capturing, compressing and recording the substantial amounts of data that this new generation of cameras creates has opened a land rush of opportunities for savvy inventors.

Panasonic HPX3000

The s.Two was essentially the first production grade, digital field recorder that made it out of the halcyon days of cinematic digital acquisition.

On location with the s.Two and the Viper.

By virtue of being the first, it is also the most field tested, and that is something you can quite literally take to the bank.

It records every camera mentioned in this book and I've even used it with the HD-SDI output of an XLH-1 with most excellent results.

The newest disk recorder to fall off of the Moore's matrix is called the Codex. It can record in a variety of formats, from two channels of HD/2K digital, all the way up to uncompressed 4K.

The Codex features removable media DiskPacks, a built-in touch-screen interface and is a very easy to use, self-contained recording system.

The Codex

Originally designed for VFX work, the RaveHD systems were used as a simple way to replace VTRs in post production. Uncompressed capture requires beef and if you want redundancy it requires even more.

RAVE Cube

As the industry began to see the advantages of direct-to-disk capture in the field, RAVE accommodated (not without a bit of kicking and screaming), by introducing a rather extensive line of disk based acquisition systems.

The largest RAVE system is called the "Monster" and records 10bit DPX files up to 4K.

The slightly bigger-than-a-football-sized RAVE-Cube is finding itself a welcome addition to a wide variety of shooting applications. Two of these systems can be linked together to create a Stereo recording system: and that is grist for another book entirely.

Representing the forward crest of the compressed recording wave, the Wafian, CineForm-based recorder can hold a day's worth of 4:4:4 HD and is easily controlled from the touch-screen on the front.

I've used this system to record VFX elements for several movies that I've served as DP on. It performed flawlessly and allowed us to keep shooting well after the tape in the Sony F-900s had run out. Plotted out on Moore's vector, the Wafian meets all the vector points except for size.

The Wafian's developer, Jeff Youel, operates on a location shoot for a feature that we're shooting about fifty yards away.

Convergent Design's Flash XDR recorder

The full clout of Moore's Law is evident in the diminutive Flash XDR recorder from Convergent Designs. Using advanced compression and storage components, this little gem records HDSDI via the camera's SDI tap. While it my not boast the storage capacity of the Wafian, it is inexpensive enough to buy several of them and swap them out to a download station when full.

LATITUDE

The single, most important thing to know about latitude is that it is the representation of the luminance value. It is the gray scale of the image, not color, that paints the play of emotions across the human face.

To put it in the context of this chapter, it is the number of gray crayons between white and black. The more latitude your camera system has, the more dynamic a performance it can capture.

Motion picture film is able to record a significantly greater range of light intensity than video. The average motion picture film stock can generally accommodate at least a ten-stop range in brightness while prosumer video is only good for a fraction of that if its lucky.

A really good, professional camcorder like an F-900 may get as much as seven stops, but it is still a limited gray scale resolution. The method with which the video industry calculates a particular camera's response to light is expressed in terms of range and graphically represented by the response curve.

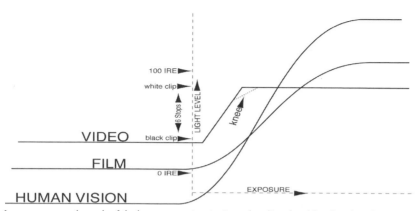

In many cameras the angle of the knee-compression circuit can be adjusted and lengthened to give even greater exposure range. With careful calibration the range of a high quality camera can be expanded almost two f stops.

The human eye can perceive an enormous range of brightness. Standing inside a house at night our eyes can make out details both within the brightly lit interior of the house as well as on its dark and shadowy exterior.

Film is not only more forgiving with high contrast ratios, but also with the way the extreme values of chroma density are handled. While video essentially clips the values that exceed its limits, film has a far more forgiving nature. At the brightest and darkest ends of the scale of illumination, film eases the values into all white or all black.

In an attempt to soften the abrupt clip levels of video the knee compression circuit, the soft clip (sometimes called *"soft shoulder"*) was devised. While it really doesn't do that much for the blacks, it has the capacity to noticeably extend the exposure range by emulating the soft shoulder of film. Many cameras have circuitry that reduces contrast by averaging the signals. While this often creates better looking video, it isn't recommended for video destined for film due to the amount of information that is discarded in the equation.

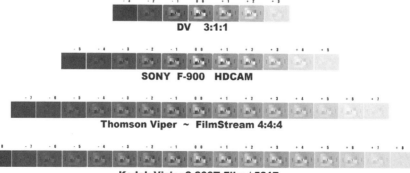

If we lay out a comparison of the latitude of the four dominant acquisition systems, they would form a pyramid. There are a lot of film emulsions, some with a lot more latitude than others, but my favorite, all-around flavor is Kodak Vision2 200T Film/5217.

Under favorable conditions you can get nearly eight stops over before the scene goes totally white and eight stops under before it goes totally black. Is this 17 stops of latitude? Technically, kind of; but in the real world, you should only count on ever using five or six of 'em.

Using the same criteria, the Viper, shooting in 4:4:4 mode, gives you 14 stops between white and black, 6-ish of them usable. 4:2:2 Sony HD-CAM gives you 10 stops between white and black and HDV gives seven.

Charts can be a bit esoteric, so I created a little test for you that is probably more relevant.

The Canon XLH-1 is used for this test because it is the first camera that technically falls into both the HDV and HD categories. Because of XLH-1's full data rate Serial Digital out, it qualifies as an HD camera, and because of its ability to record native HDV to a MiniDV cassette, it is a solid HDV contender.

Living in the netherworld between professional and consumer markets, the XLH-1 is a bit of an anomaly. The only shorcoming of the XLH-1 is the lens. By HDV standards it is absolutely awesome but in the world of high-end professional production, it just barely breaks the OK barrier.

None of the camera's native lenses would allow a ten-stop bracket, so I used a series of Formatt ND filters to help me carry the range.

If you'll pardon a second or two of soap-box time, the only reason you should ever invest in a matte box for your camera is if you intend to get serious about filtration. Without that specific caveat, matte boxes are an expensive, and somewhat ersatz, affectation.

In nearly all cases, the lens hood that shipped with the camera is better at cutting stray light. OK, I'm stepping off now.

Since the same exact image is being sent to the tape and the HD-SDI port, it is a really great way to get a head-to-head comparison between HDV's 4:2:0-ish ~ 3:1:1-ish color space and HD-SDI's 4:2:2.

I give it eight stops max: four over, four under. But really five stops — two over, two under — of usable.

Marketing departments would probably give it ten. Engineers would give it four.

Here is a web address where you can go to get a couple of these frames to try this for yourself: *www.PixelMonger. com/DGA-lat.html.* Open the image in Photoshop and go to IMAGE > ADJUSTMENTS > LEVELS.

What you'll get is a control box that illustrates the Histogram. It is a visual representation of the voltage potential of your image.

Think of the box as your bandpass, the limits of the voltage potential of your signal. It is essentially the size of your box of crayons. Black on the left, white on the right: that's your LATITUDE.

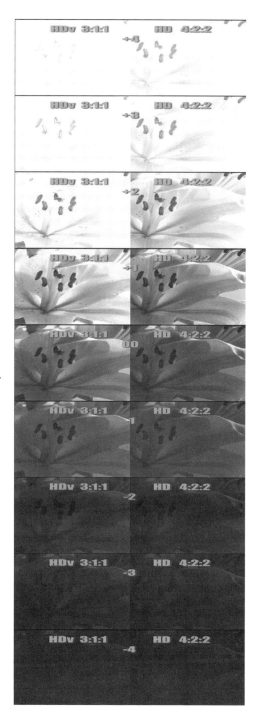

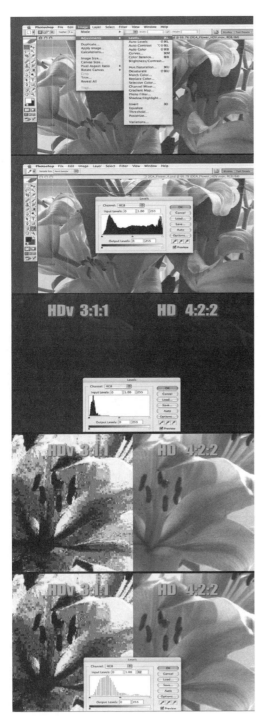

Imagine that this box is the number and value of gray crayons between white and black.

The vertical component is the voltage across the chip. In most professional diagnostic systems there are four of these for every image: RED, GREEN, BLUE and LUMINANCE.

The black image in the middle of this strip is our four-stop under image from the previous page.

See how the voltage potential is all crammed over on the left? We seem to have thrown away a lot of gray crayons.

By moving the white triangle over to the foot of the image register, we can force a new latitude profile on the image. This is one of the recovery hacks in color timing.

There, now the entire voltage of the image has been forced into a new gamma.

If you reopen the Levels control again you'll notice spaces between the black vertical lines. Those are missing crayons.

We haven't really increased the number of crayons but rather spread out the crayons that we have left to fill the box.

DIGITAL OFF-ROADING

Native HD is a rather bland affair. The factory presets are designed so that the camera performs well in a wide number of lighting and production environments. Manufacturers must take into account that since this is a cinematic production tool, the signal must be configurable to a wide range of distribution modalities, and this is where it gets confusing.

The latitude, color space and gamma curve all transpose well to the broadcast 601 standard. HD destined for digital projection however, needs to have special attention paid to resolving the denser areas as well as a few contrast management issues.

HD that is destined to be printed to film differs depending on just how you're printing and what kind of hoops you intend on making your signal jump through.

Let's face it, if you use a Sony DigiBeta or a Panasonic DVCPRO, you can rest assured that basically anything you shoot is going to look really good on a television. The cameras were made for broadcast, the factory presets are all dedicated to jumping through SMPTE hoops and I've yet to hear a dissenting voice with regard to the signal integrity of any of them in conventional video production.

HD on the other hand, especially 24P, is an image spec that is destined for a myriad of distribution modalities. Are you shooting your HD for network broadcast, or satellite distribution in MPEG, or DVD-ROM? Perhaps a theatrical release is in your plans? If so, are you planning on printing your HD to film using an intermediate stock on a laser recorder or camera stock using a Celco?

Maybe you're planning on a digital projection. Will that be using a DLP, LCD or light valve technology? Maybe online distribution is in your futurewith H.264 or one of the Wavelet flavors.So many choices, and every single one of them requires a different kind of signal. A different box of crayons, if you will.

The HD equipment manufactures are all faced with the same problem: with HD being distributed in more than a dozen different ways, what constitutes an appropriate factory preset?

The image that comes directly out of a professional HD camera via the HD-SDI (Serial Digital Interface) connector will look crisp and full on both the waveform monitor and vectorscope.

It is very important to keep in mind that this image essentially represents only the factory preset. We're using the Adobe PhotoShop Histogram to illustrate this point, but all professional graphics applications have this capability.

The same camera, chart and lighting set-up is used for all three shots. Notice how nice and *middle-of-the-road* the top image is; not just in the visual spectrum, but all the way down to the binary essence of the signal. The space to the left and right of the data group represents unused bandpass, which in this case is a bit more than 20%.

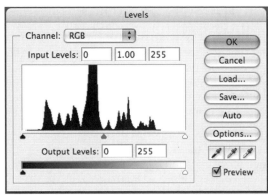

This is the histogram of a DSC chart that was shot using the Sony F900's factory presets.

With an HD signal that is destined for NTSC, this is not such a big deal because parameters for broadcast greatly truncate the edges of the voltage potential.

While you might not see the difference if you were to display this on a monitor, when projected or printed to film there is a notable variation. In post-production your keys will be nearly 20% cleaner when using a signal that was expanded or "painted" in the acquisition stage.

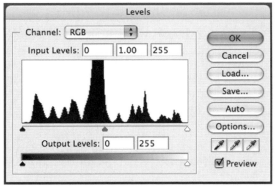

This histogram is from a chart that was timed or "painted" using the F900's Matrix adjustments and a WFM. Notice how much wider the signal is. It has significantly more usable dynamic information in it than with the factory preset signal.

The histogram is not an approximation: it is an exact reproduction of the data that it is fed.

By timing in post you get a signal that looks better to the eye but is technically inferior.

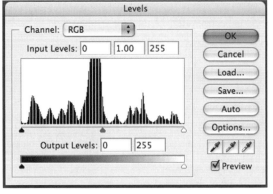

This is the histogram of the factory preset signal after it was timed in post. Notice that the envelope is almost exactly the same as the ainted histogram but the white vertical bands represent missing data.

There are a number of indispensable color management tools on the desktop.

Apple's COLOR is hard to beat for sheer power and ease of use. By timing the image stream into the groove of the basic look, you can save enormous amounts of time in post.

With cameras such as the Viper that have the capability to shoot uncorrected raw 4:4:4, the Apple's COLOR allows you to dial up a wide range of looks to satisfy even the most discerning eye.

Once reserved for only the most high-end systems, a number of very professional camera control applications are appearing on the market.

Canon's Console software controls the Canon line of cameras through a IEEE1394(FireWire) cable and provides on-screen diagnostics and calibration.

Canon's Console application loads onto your PC or Mac and controls all of the camera's functions including gamma, master pedestal, color phase, and even zoom, focus, shooting mode and frame rate. It also provides controls for direct disk recording of both the HDV and the HD-SDI image streams.

After using it on a number of projects we've found that it increases the quality of both the HD-SDI and the HDV images at least 20%.

All professional cameras incorporate some sort of ability to time the look to a profile that will allow you to take away less in post. The trick with HDV cameras is to find systems that allow you the same control.

COLOR SPACE

Color space is a mathematical model used to describe and visualize color. It is the number of different colored crayons in your box.

There are probably as many different color spaces as there are methods of creating or displaying an image. CRT monitors use one color space while LCD monitors use another. Macs are different from PCs and there are hundreds of different color spaces to accommodate the eve-expanding universe of acquisition, recording and display devices.

The vast majority of professional electrical cinematography cameras use a system of three sensor chips to record the image. Each CCD records the luminance value of the red, green and blue colors of the visible spectrum. This gives us a rather flat, greenish-looking image called raw RGB.

The Viper camera in Dual HD-SDI FilmStream mode records a raw RGB image that many people find quite objectionable. I've posted a raw RGB frame at: *www.pixelmonger.com/rawrgb.html*

Truth is, that is the way the world really looks. It is only by virtue of the unique system of rods and cones in the human retina that we see the world the way we do.

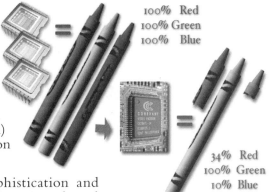

Every system that records an image must make some sort of attempt at correcting that image to meet with human standards. Electronically this is done by filtering the raw RGB using an A/D (analog to digital) converter in combination with the decoder.

100% Red
100% Green
100% Blue

34% Red
100% Green
10% Blue

Depending on the sophistication and quality of the system in question, the color space is translated into a Y'CbCr configuration. Color characteristics are then laid out in either Linear, Log or Gamma profiles that establish chroma values in concordance to standardized CIE values.

To view a specific color space within various environments (LCD vs. CRT for example) you need to apply a CLUT or Color Look Up Table to it which is essentially a magic decoder ring that tells the various colors how much they need to change their white value (white point), bit depth and chromaticity to appear as the original.

4:4:4 CRY'N OUT LOUD

The majority of professional HD cameras use three CCDs to acquire the signal. It is as though the chips give us three really big crayons with which to draw our world. One Red crayon, one Green crayon and one Blue crayon combine to create an image called RGB. It comprises equal amounts of red, green and blue data which, when combined, create a very large data stream known in geek-dom as 4:4:4.

Graphic computers operate in an RGB, 4:4:4 color space, and since all digital cameras are technically computer peripherals, full bandwidth RGB makes the optimum production format. But RGB is huge.

Human vision is far more sensitive to changes in luminance than it is to color so we can discard an enormous amount of color and get an image that still looks *good to the eye* as long as we keep the same amount of crayons between black and white (latitude).

First we need to transpose the really big RGB crayons into a more divisible unit that also breaks out the luminance values of the image. Y'CbCr does exactly that.

"Y" represents the luminance value or inherent light range of the image while Cb and Cr represent the two color values. (Cb) is BLUE MINUS LUMINANCE and (Cr) is RED MINUS LUMINANCE. Since Y encompasses R, G and B, the equation (Cr + Cb = G) will yield G (Green).

We can still have a Y'CbCr, 4:4:4 signal but it is really a different type than the one we had with RGB and takes up less than 30% of the space.

Instead of representing equal samples of red, green and blue, the new Y'CbCr, 4:4:4 represents Luminance and two color values. Although it doesn't have the full spectral range, it covers skin tones, blue sky, water and green grass quite well.

Y'CbCr also does a fairly good job at fire and explosions so, between skin and explosions, you've basically got the majority of cinema covered.

While we're on the topic, there is no such thing as digital YUV or YPbPr, or Y, B-Y, R-Y; these are all vestigial remnants of the analog age. Digital is either RGB or Y'CbCr.

If we take our Y'CbCr 4:4:4 signal and cut the amount of color down by half we end up with a 4:2:2 image where the luminance (the first number) is still represented by its full value and the two color values are each reduced by half.

A 4:1:1 signal would has full luminance but only a quarter of the original Y'CbCr color value and only 8% of the original RGB color. For every four samples of luminance there is only one sample of color. How effective is this system? 4:1:1 and its evil twins 4:2:0 and 3:1:1 are what a majority HDV and low-end HD formats consist of.

COLOR SAMPLING   *L = LUMINANCE*
                                    C = CHROMINANCE

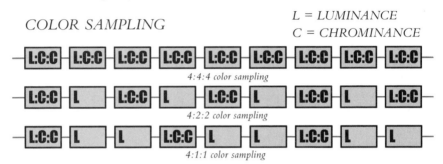

4:4:4 color sampling

4:2:2 color sampling

4:1:1 color sampling

While this color reduction is generally not visible when viewed on your home TV (which is what it is designed for), it is an almost insurmountable loss if you're trying to pull a chroma-key or project it on a theatre screen.

If you intend on doing effects or color timing in post, you'll obviously want to use a format that gives you the most color.

THROW ANOTHER LOG/LIN ON THE FIRE

There is perhaps no other aspect of motion imaging that is more open to lively discussion than the relationship between logarithmic and linear color spaces.

Without going into some very complex descriptions, let's imagine that the little sharpener that comes on the back of our very largest box of crayons is your lin-to-log converter. Camera sensors are nearly all linear. They produce three very large, very blunt, RGB crayons.

If you sharpen your blunt (LINEAR) crayon you'll get a finer image pitch at the point (LOG) with which you are able to draw a more exacting picture.

As one would imagine with a sharpener of any type, the lin-to-log conversion is destructive in that there is a good deal more information in the linear data set than in the sharpened log set.

Color correction, whether done in camera, during transfer or in post, works best on linear data (fat crayons), where your red, green and blue crayons are all represented in equal amounts.

Since color correction is sometimes even more destructive than the A/D conversion or lin-to-log conversion, it makes good sense to do it on the biggest data set possible

Cameras like the Thomson Viper have a 12-bit A/D converter from the analog CCD signal (4:4:4 RGB) which is translated into 10-bit log in FilmStream mode. Once you're into your computer, you can put the video into floating point (elastic crayon box that can accommodate any number or size of crayons) and change between log, lin and video gamma without perceptible loss.

It is in the camera, where you're recording to a specific bit depth that the most care needs to be taken. Even though the Viper creates one of the cleanest images of any camera on the market, there is still a bit of noise in this transposition.

To this, Thomson's Jan van Rooy added, *"I think the concept of (inherent) noise in imaging systems should be addressed because it is actually the shotnoise in the sensors that allows the lin-to-log conversion with negligible loss of information. Not only is noise unavoidable, but it is your friend in these cases as it allows us to see between the quantisation levels."*

Since there really isn't any practical way to get around the A/D conversion that happens in the camera head, most modern cameras offer varying levels of color value indexing.

Each crayon is 10% darker or lighter than the crayon next to it.

Let's say we were to represent the gamma or potential latitude of an image as having eleven crayons between white and black. If we considered our black crayon to have 0% luminance and then progressively added a steady 10% of luminance to the next ten crayons, we would end up with a linear progression of luminance values that would result in our white crayon at a level of 100%.

Although this is a nice, orderly system, and very easy to visualize, it is wasteful when applied to contemporary imaging technologies. Many of the gradations near the middle of the gamma can be quite easily achieved by combining different crayons.

What is needed is more information at the two extremes of the luminance set where images have a habit of crushing (blacks) and blowing out (whites).

Contrast is the culprit here, and nearly everything you do to an image adds it. By decreasing the rate of change at the white and black extremes of our little set of crayons, we are *stretching* the blacks and providing a *knee* or *roll-off* to the whites. Hopefully, this will convey far more information, through many more generations and transpositions than a straight write out of the A/D converter would allow.

SUPER CRAYON

As the name implies, *color space* is a multidimensional structure. If we were to plot out the entire visible spectrum (called CAP-XYZ or CIE XYZ), it would look like a cylinder that has been cut off at an angle.

Since color space is a naturally occurring event with direct ties to a thermonuclear event happening a few bazillion miles away, the actual dimensions are a bit more curvy than my home-made illustration would suggest. Unlike the organic shape of the visible spectrum, RGB is entirely man-made and exists as a parallelogram that fits neatly within the CAP-XYZ 3Dspace. Y'CbCr is also a man-made construct and floats within the RGB 3space.

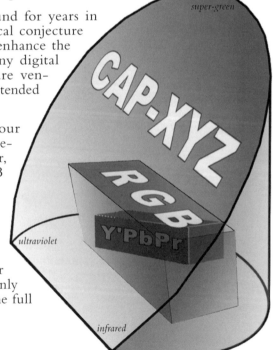

CAP-XYZ has been around for years in white papers and theoretical conjecture but lately, in an effort to enhance the cinematic experience, many digital projector manufacturers are venturing into the realm of extended color space.

If we were to imagine our CAP-XYZ color-space represented as a giant, multi-color, truncated column, the RGB colorspace would float inside taking up a bit less than 50% of the available space.

Inside the RGB cube would be floating our Y'CbCr color space, which would only account for about 14% of the full CAP-XYZ spectrum.

Even the best and biggest, full sample, 4:4:4, Y'CbCr color space image from the most technologically advanced cameras can only contain a smidgen of the available image potential.

RGB color space is based on the amount of color that a prototype Kodak film stock could record back in the 1930s. Chances are good that your grandparents weren't even born yet.

Any time you get the feeling that technology is out of control, just consider that the universal unit of measure for capturing and reproducing image is based on a prototype color film stock from back when biplanes and zeppelins were considered modern transportation. RGB is old and tired. CAP-XYZ, on the other hand, encompasses the entire visible spectrum from infrared to ultraviolet.

Why should we be concerned about expanded color space in a day when more content is viewed on handheld devices than in movie theaters?

Go in tight on a beautiful face and you'll only record a fraction of what's there. Subtleties such as the sub-surface scattering of light and the almost imperceptible blush of changing emotions are almost entirely lost with RGB.

While nearly every *advancement* in digital acquisition is aimed at reducing the size of the data set, I think we also need to champion the concept of increasing quality.

For those of you who would like to know more about the technical aspects of color space, I invite you to wander around inside the head of the most brilliant video engineer I know, Charles Poynton at: *www.poynton.com/Poynton-video-eng.html.*

While you're in there, kick him in the hypothalamus and tell him I said "Hi."

SAMPLE RATE

To continue our "box of crayons" analogy, SAMPLE RATE is the texture of an actual crayon in the box. The greater the number of times a second that the system samples "reality," the more information it contains, the larger the crayon becomes and the more accurately it can draw the image. In much the same way audio is sampled, image is also sampled.

Consider the visual component as the transposition of the analog voltage off of a camera's CCD chips into a series of digital values.

The more samples there are per second, the higher the number of bits the image data can be resolved into and the closer it comes to representing reality. Seemed simple and straightforward enough.

Then I met Stephen Hawking

Aside from being one of the most inspirational people you could ever have the good fortune to hang out with, he is also the smartest.

We found ourselves working together on a show for the Discovery Channel and in the course of that project he challenged nearly everything I held as fact about capturing what we perceive as reality.

What follows is my interpretation and translation of his explanation of how sampling works in a Native Perturbation (P-brane) existence.

The author "samples" Stephen Hawking.

If the first couple paragraphs are a good enough explanation for you, then please feel free to move on to the next chapter.

Many of Stephen's explanations dealt with the relation between ultra-violet and infra-red cut-offs in the AdS-CFT correspondence which uses Super-gravity (M-theory) as the local description of the universe.

M-theory provides for an almost infinite number of solutions and *"compactifications"* (his word, not mine) which seem to be comparable to some of the newer Wavelets compression algorithms such as CineForm.

The Wavelets systems, like the very simple form that is used in TiVo, use a scalable compression scheme to accommodate and re-contextualize observed variations in 4Space.

For instance, a sound wave isn't really "a" wave but rather an endless succession of smaller and smaller perturbations that interact with our four-dimensional world.

One interpretation is similar to the "Butterfly Effect" in chaos theory, where seemingly small variations in a system can have a ripple effect on subsequent events that may seem unrelated.

To relate this to digital acquisition, and in particular to the Sony F-900 which I used to record Stephen, both sound and image are observed by the system as a series of analog wave structures.

The most common method for illustrating wave structures such as sound waves is by using some sort of sine illustration. This illustrative shorthand conveys a good approximation of relative amplitude variations but tends to give a very two-dimensional representation of something that exists in a 4D world.

It is like tracing the outline of the Himalayan mountain range from the space shuttle. You only get a general, rather smooth interpretation of the otherwise uneven topography, because mountains, both in front and behind, are obscuring the true dynamics of the mountain range.

Himalayas

Nearly any attempt to illustrate a wave looks like a solid density image because each perturbation would be spawning an endless succession of its own perturbations. To greatly simplify this concept, a single waveform would look something like a random succession of Christmas trees sacked end to end.

From a distance this chain of Christmas trees would look like a smoothly undulating series of dynamic expressions, but upon closer examination you'd see that they are really a series of smaller and smaller discrete events, like the needles on the trees. Upon closer examination you would see the texture of the needles and the cells of the texture.

Upon even closer examination you would begin to see continuing levels of perturbations or waves, and then another and another, continuing down to the level of strings.

What this all translates to is that no matter how accurately we sample image or sound, we can only offer a rough approximation of our 4Space reality.

As a much easier example to understand and explain, let's pick a piece of the outline of a single image event. Sine we're not about to try to sample it beyond our limits of comprehension, we'll basically pick some average points along its path (samples) and then connect the dots.

Sample Rates

HDV   Broadcast   Viper

The more dots we use to sample the image or sound, the closer it comes to recreating the original but it can never be equal to the original unless you sample at the sub-atomic level.

There simply is no such thing as UNCOMPRESSED which, in the context of image and video, means that there is approximately the same number of ones and zeros in the data set as there were when it was originally written (recorded). Compression is relative only when used in context.

The chrominance of HDV is generally sampled at 3.75 MHz while cameras like the F-900 sample the chrominance at 74.25MHz/10bit, and the Viper samples all three primaries in the 74 MHz range.

Here are two HD images. The top is a .dpx frame from a Viper in FilmStream mode and the bottom one is a .mpg frame from the Sony HVRV1U HDV camcorder. They are both 1920x1080 pixels.

The Viper frame weighs in at a respectable 7.9 MB while the HDV weighs in at 150 KB. Both frames could be called *uncompressed* by enthusiastic marketing departments.

A 1080x1920 frame of raw HD, sampled at a relatively low rate of 75Mhz (Viper) is roughly 8 MB per frame. The miniDV cassette that HDV generally writes to can hold a little over 12 GBs of data. Without a lot of very complex math you wouldn't even hold a minute of HD on an entire HDV tape.

COMPRESSION

A number of people have asked why compression isn't included as one of the descriptors of HD. There are a lot of things that are far more important to the look and feel of an image than compression.

Compression is simple math. People read articles and ads and glossy brochures and memorize the compression ratios like baseball stats. Compression ratios are cocktail conversation out here in Hollywood.

Compression also makes good grist for the marketing and advertising folks because while the average consumer won't understand color space, latitude, sample rate or data rate, they can generally understand the basics of compression. A 2:1 compression ratio seems obviously better than a 20:1 ratio.

> A suitcase packed by a four-year-old is a lot less efficient than a suitcase packed by a mom.

A suitcase packed by a four-year-old is a lot less efficient than a suitcase packed by a mom. The thing that everyone gets wrong is that compression is quantitative more than it is qualitative.

There are hundreds of ways to compress a video image, some far less destructive than others. An often overlooked attribute of compression artifacts is that they are relative to image size. A compression artifact that might be heinous at standard def, could very well become invisible at 2K.

Let's take a look at a box of crayons and figure out some ways that we can make it smaller. Right off the top we see a yellow crayon. Since we have master red, blue and green crayons, we can mathematically subtract blue from green and get yellow.

So now we can pull the yellow crayon out of the box and substitute it with some simple math that only takes up the amount of space of the writing on the crayon label. If we add that little yellow formula to red, we'll get orange, so now we can throw the orange crayon away and substitute it with a tiny compound formula.

Next thing you know, we're throwing away nearly all of the crayons and substituting them for tiny little formulas. Quite space saving and not destructive at all.

How many times have you ever used a whole crayon? Probably never. Seems like there's a lot of space that is taken up by the parts of the crayon that we're really never going to use. What if we represent that mass, let's say 80% of the crayon, with a formula that says, pretend that there is a shaft here that looks exactly like the shaft of the red, green and blue crayons.

You now have two choices: you can drastically reduce the size of the box or you can put a lot more of these truncated crayons in the box you have. Keep in mind that these crayons are only good for limited "consumer" use.

If you try to use them to draw a huge "professional" mural, you'll soon run out of actual crayon and start getting into the area that is only represented by a mathematical formula. Again we have a great space savings and no real degradation of image quality unless we use these special "consumer" crayons for something they weren't designed for.

What if we shrank the crayons down and made them really, really skinny? They might break easier and they won't last nearly as long, but they sure would take up much less space.

Obviously the line they draw is a lot thinner, so we would need to move our hand a lot faster to cover the same area as we would with a fat crayon. Looking at the final image though, it is identical to the one made with the fat crayons. In the right situation, and using the correct methodology, we can save enormous space while creating a very similar image.

I have yet to find an area of digital acquisition that can't be covered by the crayon analogy. Perhaps we did learn everything we need to know in kindergarten.

I've tried to keep everything rather simple in this book because, let's face it, digital is inherently simple. Compression based on simple math is also quite simple.

JPG, MPG and the half dozen clonettes of their mathematical shell game siblings have kept us all amused with their various ratios and permutations since the very first pixels crested the binary horizon.

Block compression schemes exploit numerical redundancy in such a way as to represent the original data set. This uncompressed string:

$$11100110000000001001001$$

... could be written as:

$$1 \; \{7\} \; 0 \; \{14\}$$

By saying there are seven ones and fourteen zeros, we maintain the intent of the original string, but it is written in a smaller form.

Using this quazi-lossless system of compression we could take a string of code that would stretch for ten miles and reduce it to less than a dozen characters.

Then there are the basic blocking compressions such as the MPEG and JPEG systems. They group pixel groups into 8 X 8 or 16 X 16 blocks and perform a form of averaging. Think of blocking compression as lots of little digital "dittos."

When you add sequential frames into the compression scheme, a whole new world of opportunities opens up. One of the most popular motion compression schemes is to write a full frame and then only write out the differences a given number of succeeding frames. Sections that may include a swath of blue sky may only need very minimal redraw while sections where one object crosses another are often prone to artifacting. And then there are Wavelets.

WAVELETS

Like many who actually work with the image from acquisition through post, I have been a long-time proponent of *no compression, anywhere in production.* Distribution however, is based on compression, so the less restructuring that the image goes through during manufacture, the better it will look on the big or small screen.

Originally a classified military formula, Wavelets was first tested with great success as the "secret ingredient" in TiVo.

There are currently two camera systems (Silicon Imaging which uses CineForm & RED which uses RED Code) that are using Wavelets as a native format. Both offer Moore's Law performance and economy.

While not as simple to explain as MPEG, Wavelets is the next, long overdue step into the future of cinema. For me, the most accurate explanation comes from my favorite astrophysicist, Amara Graps.

"The fundamental idea behind wavelets is to analyze according to scale. Indeed, some researchers in the wavelet field feel that, by using wavelets, one is adopting a whole new mind-set or perspective in processing data.

"Wavelets are functions that satisfy certain mathematical requirements and are used in representing data or other functions. This idea is not new. Approximation using superposition of functions has existed since the early 1800s, when Joseph Fourier discovered that he could superimpose sines and cosines to represent other functions. However, in wavelet analysis, the scale that one uses in looking at data plays a special role.

"Wavelet algorithms process data at different scales or resolutions. If we look at a signal with a large 'window,' we would notice gross features. Similarly, if we look at a signal with a small 'window,' we would notice small discontinuities. The result in wavelet analysis is to "see the forest and the trees.

"For many decades, scientists have wanted more appropriate functions than the sines and cosines which comprise the bases of Fourier analysis, to approximate choppy signals. By their definition, these functions are non-local (and stretch out to infinity), and therefore do a very poor job in approximating sharp spikes. But with wavelet analysis, we can use approximating functions that are contained neatly in finite domains. Wavelets are well-suited for approximating data with sharp discontinuities."

Amara Graps, PhD

Want more? www.amara.com/current/wavelet.html

My good friend Mike Most has a very practical take on Wavelets. Since he is primarily concerned with visual effects and post production, his concerns tend to deal with the day-to-day performance in a high-end, cinematic context.

"The use of high efficiency wavelet codecs, and their application to camera raw data, is clearly an approach that works, as shown by both Red and Cineform. Anyone who sees wavelets footage and understands what it is they are seeing would have to come away with some degree of doubt that uncompressed is the only route to quality imagery at high resolutions.

"If quality can be preserved, and the fine detail that can only be had with high resolution capture can be maintained, then what exactly is the problem with utilizing properly done compression technology to allow us to do this with today's processing and storage equipment? Sure, you still need to be monitoring all of this properly, and have a proper color management scheme in place to ensure calibration, and there is still the need to conform to standards on the post end (DCI, for instance). After what I've seen, my feeling is that compression − properly implemented − is your friend, in the same way that nonlinear editors became your friend.

"Why record on stacks of hard drives connected by a fat cable if you can get essentially identical results by recording on a self contained, mountable recording medium that costs a lot less and holds a lot more? While it's true there's no free lunch, it now appears to me like there is at least a free snack, as long as you watch what you eat." ~ Mike Most

CHAPTER 5

THE FLAVORS OF HD

Choosing the right tool with which to tell your tale is one of the more confusing aspects of digital production. With film, it's a relatively easy decision. Budget, format, crew, and location all conspire to give you two or three basic choices, which are then narrowed down by personal preference.

Marshall McLuhan put it quite simply when he observed: *We shape our tools and they in turn shape us.*

In the film world there exists a methodology that has changed little in the past century. An enhanced level of professionalism has taken advertising hype out of the decision-making process because manufacturers assume that the vast majority of cinematographers have already been shaped by their tools.

The industry's slow growth allowed parallel systems to evolve. The same piece of 35mm film fits into a 1949 Mitchell BNC or a 2009 Panavision Millennium.

There are many different camera manufacturers, all catering to different preferences based on what you shot and where you lived. 8mm for consumers, 16mm for industrial and independents and 35mm for features. This very simple system worked for over a hundred years.

"Just as the wheel is an extension of the leg, and radio is an extension of the voice, so too is the camera an extension of the eye, the computer an extension of the brain, and wiring, circuits, and the internet an extension of the nervous system." As Steve Mann suggests in his Keynote Address at the McLuhan Symposium on Culture and Technology, your tools are an extension of your body and mind.

Panavision, Arriflex, Aaton, Cinema Products took the high ground with other smaller manufacturers picking up the niche markets of high-speed, ultra-light weight, underwater, stunt and so on. All in all, a rather mellow, high-quality field of competition. Then came HD.

The only way to evaluate what tools are right for you is to poke around and try them yourself. Which tools do you feel are destined to become an extension of your body?

My good friend Sean Fairburn has one of the more homespun points of view with regard to HD and I get a chuckle every time I hear him describe it.

"I come from southern Louisiana where fresh water and salt water meet in the bayous. It's neither fresh nor salt, but rather a combination of both that's called brackish water," he says with his southern drawl.

"In my opinion, 24p HD is similar to brackish water in that it's neither film nor video. It exists in both worlds simultaneously. In interlace mode, it's really, really good video — better than anything out there. In progressive mode, it's darn near indistinguishable from film, but it's also a heck of a lot cheaper and a heck of a lot faster with the added advantage of being able to see exactly what you're getting." ~ Sean Fairburn SOC

B. Sean Fairburn SOC.

As with so many of our tools that have survived the digital revolution, advanced motion imaging isn't as much about the hardware anymore as it is about breaking through the media clutter that surrounds it. With almost a hundred flavors of HD to choose from, the need for context is a lot more important than a handful of glossy brochures full of technical buzzwords.

The esoteric mumbo-jumbo and guesswork has been taken out of the cinematic process. Of course it has been replaced with a lot of technical mumbo-jumbo, but the cool thing about this post–digital age is that the key to success is not as dependent on understanding how something works. All you need to know is what it does.

For most, the actual decision of which format and computer platform to go with comes down to a subtle mélange of McLuhanesque influences and the price/performance ratio. What is the most affordable system and methodology that has a chance of becoming a natural extension of your being?

Technically you need to consider signal quality, latitude, color space and data rates. Humanistically you need to consider controls, features, form factor, weight, design and ergonomics. Computer platform decisions should concern ease of use, selection of software applications, data rates and cost factors.

Every aspect of design can be used to trigger emotional connections. Every aspect of signal quality can be used like a game of Three-Card Monty. What might sound like the best quality based on compression might actually not be the best based on data rates.

While I obviously can't crawl inside your head and help you with emotional and psychological decisions, I can help you with the technical ones.

Obviously, you want to use the highest resolution that you can afford, but there's a whole lot more to resolution than just the number of pixels on your CCD chip. Digital acquisition is a process, and the images must pass through a number of hurdles.

If you hook the video out from a number of different cameras to identical video monitors, they'll all give you a relatively nice image.

What you don't see is what that image looks like once it is recorded. Different formats may suffer due to inferior electronics or poor lenses. The actual speed of the tape or disk/RAM packing structure has an effect upon the signal's integrity, as does the method employed to record color and luminance information.

> **Every aspect of design can be used to trigger emotional connections.**

Taking this all into consideration, why would you want to go through all the trouble of making a movie (which, by the way, stands a very good chance of being the only movie you'll ever make) on an obviously inferior format?

As long as you have freedom of choice, exercise it. And most importantly, don't believe any salesmen, advertisements, articles or books (even mine) that offer a quick and painless solution.

Marshall McLuhan was often referred to as the "Oracle of the Electronic Age." His fundamental belief in technological determinism is one of the central themes of his best-selling book *The Medium Is the Massage* (no, that's not a misspelling, he just had a whack sense of humor). In it he proposed the notion that the message is greatly impacted by the delivery system. In his view, *how* we say something is more important that *what* we say.

He divided content into two distinct categories, *hot* and *cold*. Hot media represented higher resolutions which lowered audience participation, while cold media (with much lower resolution) causes the audience to fill in missing information and thereby become participatory. To me, the cinematic dividing line between hot and cold media is HDV/HD. What is it to you? Do you favor hot or cold media?

PROSUMER VS. PROFESSIONAL

There is a billion-dollar industry invested in having you believe that miniDV formats such as HDV are professional formats.

I just got back from the Sundance Film Festival where I watched an otherwise decent movie get jeered because the quality of the projected image was so bad. Aside from some remedial camera work, they had done everything else well enough, but since they were using HDV, there wasn't enough data in the master to color correct and still have a projectable image.

Perhaps if they had taken the time to match the shots and scenes when they were shooting them they wouldn't have had such wide discrepancies in the look and feel. It might have been a totally different experience for them.

Just because it looks good on a computer monitor, doesn't mean a thing when it comes to a full theatrical projection.

I was standing in the back of the theatre next to the one-and-only Harvey Weinstein as we watched their screening deteriorate. Harvey even held the door open for me as we both snuck out. With the door closing behind us he turned, shook his head and said, *"When will they learn?"* Harvey went on to buy seven movies at Sundance for a total of $22 million. If the filmmakers had used a decent camera, or even good methodology, they probably would have been one of them.

Without a long and successful career to back up your format decisions, everything you do is going to be judged on its professionalism. The format that you choose to work with will speak volumes.

From HDV to professional HD, the choices are endless. Like any determination regarding major investments, you want to make your decision based on qualified and quantifiably sound information.

This is a gross over-simplifica-tion, but there are basically two flavors of HD. What you call it it depends on what you're selling. but basically, the growing con-sensus seems to be settling in on calling them HD and HDV.
One way to tell them apart is by the way they transfer their signals.

If it uses a BNC to transfer the HD-SDI signal, it is a professional HD system. If it uses IEEE-1394 protocol over FireWire, it is a prosumer HDV system.

THE AMERICAN SYNDROME

The most rudimentary problem with moviemakers emerging from the world of HDV is this uniquely American predisposition to own everything you use. Perhaps it's a result of living in the most media-saturated country in the world, but the urge to own is an entirely inappropriate concept for motion picture production.

Geoff Boyle, FBKS

I know quite literally hundreds of cinematographers, but few have put back into the industry like the noted British cinematographer Geoff Boyle. If you want a crisp vision of the level of quality and integrity that you should be aspiring to, check out his site *(www. cinematography.net/geoff)*. If you have questions with regard to cinematic technique, methodology or technology, check out the adjacent CML resource which he founded and is internationally regarded as the definitive last word.

Being a no-nonsense Brit, a truly great cinematographer and a person who has been through the equipment-owning aspects of production for many years, I asked him to contribute a summery of his experience with respect to ownership.

"I've owned or part-owned kit for the last 25 years. This has included the original Sony tube cameras, 1" portable recorders, the first Betacams, the first CCD Betacams, the first of the one-piece Betacams and the last Betacam that Thomson made — in all, around 10 top-of-the-range broadcast cameras; there have also been Aaton LTRs and XTRs, as well as an Arri 435 along the way.

"The video cameras never made much money. They basically just paid for the next generation in an area where a two-year-old camera is obsolete.

"The film cameras made money because they have a much longer write-off period, but not the kind of money you'd like to make.

"The problem is that most people don't cost camera ownership accurately, because once you've got the camera you need all the other bits that people expect you to have and not charge extra for, and don't forget insurance! My current insurance bill is $11,000 per annum.

"Let the rental companies take the risk on the major items.

"If you have money to invest in kit, then spend it on the specialist bits that rental houses don't carry and that you can charge an outrageous amount of money for. In terms of return on investment, my 15-way VGA splitter is the most profitable piece of kit I've ever owned, it's returned its cost 20 times. Specialist lenses are good as well. One of my ACs bought his own wireless focus and now has three, as they were so popular.

"It's easy to do the math: cost of kit and upkeep and insurance and transport and storage of kit, expected life of kit, return on sale of kit when obsolete, daily hire rate you can expect for kit, hassle of collecting that rate, bad debts.

"Buy equipment that you can rent/use long term, lenses are particularly good in this respect." ~ Geoff Boyle FBKS

So, unless you are a well-respected cinematographer, who shoots as your primary occupation, knows damn near everyone in the business and are known and respected for the excellence of your craft ... well, then maybe you should just rent.

TOP TEN REASONS TO RENT

01–It's the professional thing to do.

02–You'll get a whole lot more resolution for your buck with renting than you ever will with purchasing.

03–You won't be constantly worried about damaging your "baby" so you'll go for more interesting shots.

04–You can upgrade your grip, gaff and lens packages with all the money you save.

05–If there's a problem, you can swap out the camera and keep shooting.

06–You've got a built-in technical support staff.

07–You'll be free to utilize the most contemporary methodology on your next movie.

08–You are assured of proper alignment and functionality.

09–Your purchase won't devaluate upwards of 70% by the time you finish your project.

10–You can continue to work toward your goal of becoming a moviemaker without the distraction of becoming a rental house.

TOP TEN REASONS TO BUY

01–You love acquiring possessions.

02–You love to tinker with stuff.

03–You think that you're being clever by getting your financial backers to buy you a camera.

04–You already know that your movie is going to suck so you're hedging your bets.

05–You secretly want to be in the equipment rental business.

06–You love having your friends constantly asking to borrow your equipment.

07–The hours you spend maintaining your gear give your pathetic life meaning.

08–You're a multimillionaire and you need the write-off.

09–Your rapidly antiquated format fulfills your need to defend lost causes.

10–It's a good conversation starter at parties.

There is a very basic assortment of tools that you should consider owning as a digital moviemaker. They are: a video graphics-capable computer, a light meter, a small lighting kit, a chart (preferably a DSC CamAlign FrontBox), a roll of chroma key fabric and an HDV camcorder to experiment with. Everything else should be rented.

EVERY BUCK YOU WASTE ON EQUIPMENT IS A BUCK THAT DOESN'T GO UP ON THE SCREEN, SO...

(1) Get your hands dirty: You can delegate the process of gathering information and trying out various systems, but you can't delegate the final decisions. Before you open the checkbook or decide on a format, at least one person whose ass is on the line needs to actually learn and understand the technologies and the basic operation of the systems that you're going to use. If you rely on a sales person or someone who isn't invested in the production, then you're too far removed and a world of pain and disappointment is waiting just around the corner. There is far too much snake oil in this industry to rely on anything but hands on, trial and error.

(2) Only buy what you need: The actual production process of a movie easily runs a year, while the time that you spend shooting generally lasts several weeks. The predisposition to purchase your camera is an affectation of advertising and that strange, predominantly male gene that loves to acquire and tinker. Get over it! You can rent an F-900 for less than a hot HDV set-up would cost and then put the extra money you save up on the screen.

(3) Buy in the *Sweet Spot*: If you absolutely feel the need to own your camera, then please have the common sense to buy in the negotiable area between too expensive and too old. Don't necessarily go for the most expensive or newest gear you can find because you're going to end up paying through the nose. Who wants to be in the middle of production when their spiffy new camcorder is recalled?

(4) Buy or rent good equipment from a quality vendor: Those deals in the back of magazines might look tempting, but where are they when your nifty new camcorder starts eating tapes for breakfast? The vast majority of individuals that rent out production packages are generally former victims of the urge to buy. They simply can't compete with the maintenance and instant replaceability of a quality vendor. Service, even for battle-weary old curmudgeons like me, is as important as the technology.

(5) Beware of buzzwords: Don't allow buzzwords to serve as verbal shortcuts until you've clearly communicated that you understand exactly what they're supposed to mean. Phrases like *"enhanced resolution"* or *"wide screen emulation"* may sound great but generally mean that the manufacturer is just trying to keep up with the market without actually improving the merchandise.

(6) Stick with the simplest technology that works for you: The whole thing about computers and digital technology is that it's supposed to make things easier, yet nearly every industry magazine spends page after page comparing tweaky little features between competing products. 90% of the people use 10% of the features of any given digital product, whether hardware or software. Let's say you have a choice between two cameras, and they both create identical images. The one with fewer features is probably not only going to save you money but will probably be far more dependable and much easier to use. You don't want to be on a hot set reading the instruction manual.

(7) Favor *proven* over *breakthrough*: After doing time out on the bleeding edge of digital production, you'll start to recognize a certain type of person who is always extolling the virtues of the *newest hardware* that's *supposed to be* better than everything else on the market. Buffer yourself from these people. Don't risk system downtime on something that isn't proven. A battle-proven system will get you to the premiere more dependably, and that is what it's all about.

(8) If it ain't broke, don't fix it: Avoid all upgrades once you're in production! The real cost of a major hardware or software upgrade is lost time and productivity. Even though the manufacturer, sales people and every magazine in the industry tell you that the new improved upgrade is ten times better, stick to the flavor that works. There is also the chance that one small, seemingly insignificant change in the linking together of disparate systems (concatenation) can have a compounding effect on the final image quality.

HD IN HOLLYWOOD

Hollywood (the hype factory) loves HD; you can read about it in every industry magazine.

Hollywood (the industrialized manufacturing center that creates a product which contributes to the GNP) runs hot and cold on the topic of HD. Mostly cold.

Everyone in Hollywood is anxious to go DIGITAL although few if any have a firm grasp of the realities involved.

If you've got the money to shoot film, in many cases, you might be far better off shooting film. Digital production, especially HD, has a wide range of advantages, but if you don't understand those advantages they all become disadvantages. Without the extreme latitude of film to cover your mistakes, you are screwed.

The motion picture manufacturers have been burned so many times that many major production companies, mini-major studios and monolithic producers have a moratorium on HD production.

It is easy to envision some big-wig producer who just saw something shot on a Viper handing over a million-dollar check to a kid who just bought a thousand-dollar HDV camcorder. They're both thinking HD, but the lack of standardization in addition to some unscrupulous advertising has made it a losing situation.

The problem is that HD is really more of a marketing term than a real production standard. This can have catastrophic effects on the career of someone foolish enough not to have a firm understanding of the digital fundamentals.

Every major and mini-major studio has a closet full of HD projects that cost millions and are un-releasable. Best guess is that there is currently well over a billion dollars of dead HD inventory sitting in Hollywood vaults.

There are hundreds of well-intentioned movie makers who have projects locked away that will never see another photon of light. As frustrating as this is for them, the studios have learned their lessons, taken the write-offs and they are not about to invest more money in something that is so ill defined.

If George Lucas, Robert Rodriquez, David Fincher or Michael Mann want to shoot in HD, no problem; safe bets all. For the rest of us though, it's an uphill battle.

The salvageability of a poorly shot film project is several orders of magnitude greater than that of a poorly shot HD project. In an atmosphere that values youthful insights and styles, acquisition systems that have the most *recoverability* in post will be the safest choices to send out with unseasoned crews.

The technical issues are only half of the problem though. HD shortcuts the upward migration to a qualified DP position in feature production. Basically any ENG (Electronic News Gathering) videographer can rent a better camera and call himself a cinematographer.

In an industry that makes far too many deals based on giving a good meeting, this can be catastrophic.

The solution seems to me, to abandon HD and all reference to it in the context of high-end, motion picture production. As a working DP I rarely if ever use the term "HD" in pitches, production meetings or any cinematic context.

Perhaps the salvation for cinematic digital acquisition lies in the new generation of 2K & 4K cameras — Dalsa, Red, Silicon Imaging, et al. are moving us away from the hype-fest of HD and into a new era of digital acquisition that is qualitatively on a par with that of film.

Nearly all production managers, producers and post-supers understand 2K in the context of digital intermediate. The comfort zone of 2K acquisition is a lot closer than the comfort zone of HD will ever be.

There is really no need for consumer camera manufacturers to start kicking out 2K or 4K equivalents of HDV because the home viewing systems are all standardizing to conventional 1080 HD.

Perhaps the murky waters of digital acquisition will clear long enough for Hollywood (the industrialized manufacturing center that creates a product which contributes to the GNP) to embrace it as the powerful tool we all know it to be.

MOORE'S LAW: By the time this book goes into its fourth edition, the industry will have standardized on using HD for consumers and 2K and 4K for professionals.

THE NEXT BIG THING

Actually, for us in the movie biz, the next big thing is really quite a small thing. Complementary-symmetry, Metal–Oxide–Semiconductor. The vast majority of the new cameras cresting the binary horizon use single CMOS chips which are digital, deliver much larger images and use less than 10% of the power of CCDs.

SiliconImaging SI-1920HDVR

Dalsa Origin

RED

Arri D-20

They also generate much larger data streams, which results in larger capture files, which then impacts the post-production workflow. Perhaps the best way to explain them is to compare them to what they will soon replace.

Just about the only thing the top four cameras in the HDV and HD categories have in common is the fact that they all use 3 Charge Coupled Devices (CCD) to acquire the image.

There have been many attempts to compare CCD and CMOS technologies, but the efforts of this book are to keep it simple. Up until now, all professional cameras had three chips, each recording the luminance value of a specific color of the visible spectrum in red, green and blue. It is as though the chips give us three crayons with which to draw our world.

100% Red
100% Green
100% Blue

34% Red
100% Green
10% Blue

To recap what we've already covered; video cameras use an analogue-to-digital converter and an encoder to truncate the image (much the way our brains do), which results in an image with only 34% of the red and 10% of the blue left.

Here you have my custom .003 mega pixel CMOS chip. Think of it as a microscopic muffin tin designed to catch photons of light.

Unlike the 3CCD system, where you have one chip for each of the RGB channels, the CMOS chip must use a filter.

There are several different ways to filter a CMOS chip but the most popular seems to be the Bayer Pattern, which uses twice as many green filter elements than red or blue. It is like giving you an extra green crayon.

Now the encoder is still going to throw away 66% of the red and nearly 90% of the blue, but since you have two greens, it needs to take less red and blue away to give you a corrected image.

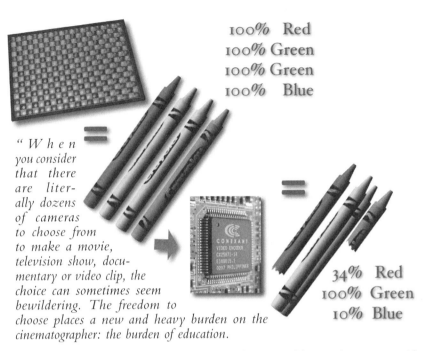

100% **Red**
100% Green
100% Green
100% **Blue**

" *W h e n*
you consider
that there
are liter-
ally dozens
of cameras
to choose from
to make a movie,
television show, docu-
mentary or video clip, the
choice can sometimes seem
bewildering. The freedom to
choose places a new and heavy burden on the
cinematographer: the burden of education.

34% **Red**
100% Green
10% **Blue**

"*The cinematographer is responsible to his director and his producers to provide the highest quality that they can afford, and his choice can make the difference between the success or failure of the project. Cameramen everywhere are now faced with the need to read about, research, and, more than anything else, understand the broad spectrum of hardware available for their work.*

"*Gone are the days when a cinematographer could walk into a meeting with a director or producer and bluff his way through a hardware discussion, only to do the minimum research required after the meeting. Perhaps the craft of cinematography once had a 'seat of the pants' aspect to it, but those days are now long gone. Cameramen are now required to be equal parts artist and technician, painter and scientist, poet and accountant.*

"*With the proper research under your belt, there will always come the same moment of truth in choosing which camera or recorder or monitor to use for any given project: 'What camera should we use?'*

"*The cinematographer that has truly done his homework and done it well can answer authentically, without an agenda. Educated and informed, he can answer the question without having to lean on his own familiarity with one camera system or another, he can answer the question by prescribing the best camera for the work, and he will always choose the absolute best quality hardware that he can possibly afford with the money the project has.*"

~ David Stump, ASC

MOORE'S LAW TODAY

So what's next? What does your next professional camera look like?

Let's go back to the basic SIZE, CAPACITY, PERFORMANCE and PRICE vectors of Moore's Law.

In a professional production environment, for general use, I find the Iconx too small ... and the Big Guys too big.

Although I love my Apple-carts, they are just too old-school. Even many of the newer disk recording systems are reaching the end of their performance vector. The next generation of recording systems will be RAM-based or disk-based systems that will be on-board.

There have been so many productions go bad over misunderstandings about the the term HD, that 2K and 4K systems will begin to dominate the market. HD is essentially dead for professional production.

Traditionally, amateurs buy, professionals rent. Big budget projects generally go with the Genesis while the darling of the low-budget world is the Varicam. The Sony F-900 is the work-horse of the industry and accounts for more HD projects I would assume, than all other HD Cameras combined. Factored into our formula, we get this:

SIZE - About the size of a football.

WEIGHT - In the ball park of a human head.

CAPACITY - At least twenty minutes to onboard RAM or disk.

PERFORMANCE - 2K / 4K systems using Wavelets Compression.

PRICE - Below the Varicam range. $20K ~ $40K, ready to shoot.

There are two, high-end, cinematic camera systems that could truly be considered in compliance with Moore's Law.

Silicon Imaging SI-2K   RED ONE

If I were to list the two smartest guys I know of with regard to compression *and* cinematic technology, one of them is working for Silicon Imaging (David Neumann) and one is working for RED (Graham Natress).

Then you've got to consider the leaders of the rebellion. At SI you've got the articulate Ari Presler running the show as CEO and at RED you've got the high-energy brilliance of Ted Schilowitz whose official title is fittingly enough, *Leader of the Rebellion.*

Silicon Imaging is a well-established industrial camera manufacturer, RED is run by Oakley sunglass founder Jim Jannard. Perhaps most interesting is that both cameras come from relatively small companies.

As discussed in the previous chapter, both cameras shoot variable bitrate, full raster, RGB, 4:4:4 Wavelet-based proprietary codecs. The SI-2K is 10 bit and the RED is 12 bit. As this book goes to press, the resolution options for the SI-2K are 720p, 1080p or 2048x1152, while the RED shoots 720p, 1080p, 1080i, 2K, 4K, 4.5K.

Both cameras use a single sensor CMOS chip with a Bayer pattern filter. The SI-2K uses an off-the-shelf, 2/3" inch 16:9 (2048x1152) Altasens HD4562 sensor. RED is not disclosing the source of their *"Mysterium"* chip but it has the same footprint as a Super35mm, 24.4x13.7mm sensor with 4520x2540 usable pixels.

Both cameras have the capability to record RAW data for higher quality needs such as visual effects. The SI uses the highest quality setting in the CineForm compression arsenal while in addition to a higher quality RAW setting, the RED uses dual HDSDI taps to send a 3Gb/sec, 4:4:4, 2K data stream out to high-end recorders.

Since these are both cinema cameras and not video cameras there really isn't as much focus on audio. SI does a track of temp audio while the RED does 4 channel uncompressed 24 bit, 48KHz.

Both systems record their big, high quality, Wavelet-compressed data streams to small, inexpensive drives. The SI-MAG drive is essentially a 2.5" SATA drive that slides into the back of the camera body. Fill it up, slam in another one and keep on shooting. Nothing proprietary, nothing fancy, you can buy more at your local computer store for $100.

The RED-DRIVE is essentially the same thing with the addition of a cool logo, matching black anodized shock case, custom connectors and mounting brackets. It has also been tested and certified and when it comes to shooting to a disk, I really don't mind the extra money for a little piece of mind. With either system, a 200GB drive can hold a good 4 hours of 2K.

The RED also has the option to record to onboard RED-RAM, or the diminutive RED-FLASH. If you flip back to the 4th page of the Moore's Law chapter, that little flash card in the vector graphic is what the RED records ten minutes of 4K to.

This *digital ravioli* is the equivalent of a 400ft. roll of 35mm film and represents the clearest example of how relevant Moore's Law is to everything we do. The RED-FLASH could very well be the technological context for this era of cinema.

The bare bones price for the cameras as depicted in the previous page is $22K for the SI-2K and $18K for the RED. No lens, no viewfinder/monitor, no recording media, no battery.

How then, can you make an intelligent decision as

Ted Schilowitz with a RED-FLASH drive.

to which camera is going to be more appropriate for your style of production?

Post workflow is where these two cameras really stand apart. The SI-2K is essentially a PC peripheral from the ground up, while the RED is a Mac peripheral through and through.

If you're a fan of Premier Pro or PC-Avid for editing, then the SI is probably the unit for you. If, like me, you're a fan of the partially eaten fruit, and FinalCut is your edit system of choice, then you're a RED fan. Since Macs can boot Windows, OSX'ers could go either way without too much discomfort.

CineForm has a QuickTime wrapper for their codec which will allow you to use SiliconImaging files on your Mac. Of course you could export RED files from the RED ALERT interface in a PC-friendly format, but gear is gear. Cameras are computer peripherals folks, there just isn't any gray area here.

As this book goes to press I'm in preproduction to direct a feature on the lot at Universal Studios. They are letting me pick the camera system and I have chosen to use a RED. This is the first time in the past twenty years that, given the choice of format, I haven't said *"Film."*

OTHER TAKES ON RED

"Shooting with RED is like hearing The Beatles for the first time. RED sees the way I see. Someday I hope to find out exactly how Jim and his team made something so technologically advanced seem so organic, so beautifully attuned to that most natural of phenomena, light. But for now I'm just glad I've got my hands on the damn thing, because it's actually making the film better because of its emotionality. At the same time, I am still figuring it out, still trying to discover its secrets, still interacting with it. For me, this is Year Zero; I feel I should call up Film on the phone and say, 'I've met someone.' Is it perfect? Not yet. But the flaws are fixable and anybody who doesn't embrace the flash-card – regardless of time restraints – is an idiot. ~ Steven Soderbergh

Jeff Kreines was the first person I know of to actually take a serious shot at building a better digital cinema camera. Readers of *Digital Moviemaking 2* will perhaps remember my enthusiasm over the diminutive Kinetta taking on the big guys.

Kreines learned a painful lesson: the problem with bleeding-edge technologies is that a single supplier's failure to deliver key parts when promised is usually fatal. The *context* of his view from the trenches gives what is perhaps the most insightful take on the RED.

"Jim has a big advantage here – RED is a small company, with small over-head (compared to Sony, or the others) – and Jim is in the unique position of not needing to make huge amounts of money off of his camera to keep afloat. He's self-funded, and sells direct – no investors to keep happy, no distributors and dealers to add to the selling price.

"It's clearly a labor of love – not a mere product.

"The RED's price point is going to scare away most competition in the 4K world – because only someone who had faith in how many cameras they could sell, and the ability to fund significant R&D, would set a price low enough that it worked only when one built significant quantities of cameras.

"Sure, you could make them out of plastic, and save a few hundred dollars, and condense the circuitry to big ASICs (but lose the ability to reformulate the camera by reprogramming the FPGAs in the field), and you could reduce the feature set – but remember, the big companies sell through distributors and dealers, so that mark-up is going to stay in place.

"While I'm sure it could happen, it would be difficult for a Sony or Panasonic to make much money on a $15,000 4K camera.

"And the pre-sale deposits were very clever – they helped define the market's size, and turned a couple thousand people into evangelists. Seemed a bit crazy at first, but a smart move.

"Anyway, while competition is always good, it's a lot easier to compete against a $100,000 camera than a $17,500 (plus accessories) camera." ~ Jeff Kreines

Almost lost in the noise that surrounds great leaps in technology are some of the more practical benefits inherent in their advanced design.

"Often overlooked in the race to spew numbers is the simple fact that compression artifacts tend to remain about the same pixel size regardless of image size. So, they generally become less significant at higher frame sizes. A compression ratio which might be unacceptable at standard def can become invisible at 4K, and so on. Also, images tend to get hurt relative to their contrast, log vs. linear, or linear light vs. print density, for instance." ~ Tim Sassoon

On August 31st. 2007, RED delivered the first batch of cameras to a hand-full of their first customers in an orientation seminar at their Orange County headquarters.

"I'd like to make it clear that the RED ONE is NOT finished. It will never be... we picked this moment in time to start sharing the everlasting development. All features are not enabled, more will be added as we go along. The image is incredible but can be made better. The accessories will evolve. You can shoot a feature right now with this camera. Ask Soderbergh. But when you try to pick it apart (I know you will)... just remember, as you discover some issue, it might have already been fixed and emailed to our customers as a firmware update. We are treating this project completely different than any I can recall. It is fluid. Just so you know. ~ Jim Jannard

Among the first cameras delivered that day were RED Cameras #24 and #25 to my good friend Dale Launer. The following day a few of us showed up on his doorstep to help him unpack.

The very first image, from the very first RED camera in Hollywood - Sept. 1st 2007

Readers of the last book in this series will remember Dale from the *Breaking out of Hollywood* chapter where he described his frustration with the Hollywood machine. In a nutshell, Dale is one of my more eccentric friends, and that's really saying something. He's written a slew of movies that you've seen and loved: *My cousin Vinny, Ruthless People, Dirty Rotten Scoundrels* to name a few.

"About six years ago I bought one of the first professional video camcorders; a Sony HDW-F900. It was simple in some ways, complicated in others. I took a three day class to explain the camera to me and I didn't understand 10% of it. Gamma? What's gamma? Isn't that what turned some guy into The Hulk?

"As I spent more time with the camera, I discovered things I liked and didn't like. One thing I never liked was the price. $93,000.00 without batteries or a lens.

"It didn't record the full 1920x1080 of the sensors, but threw away 25% so the data stream could be shrunk to a more manageable size, and then it was compressed. I wanted more. I was craving pixels. So like a few other people, I started to muse about a dreamcam.

"I did this musing online hoping someone somewhere will listen and run with it. Instead of a prism and three sensors, why not use a single sensor like we see with digital SLRs? No prism means it could be made cheaper, lighter and smaller. And with a single plane to focus on, you could use motion picture lenses, which were also a smaller, cheaper, and a little faster. Now this is getting interesting. And instead of that bulky tape system - just use a hard drive. A hard drive is smaller, collects data faster, costs less per gigabyte of storage than tape. Again, the camera could be made cheaper and smaller. And eventually you will be able to record to solid state; no hard drive, no moving parts.

"Well, the Doubting Thomases came out swinging and saying it couldn't be done. My life has been full of Doubting Thomases and when they say it can't be done I say "Wow! It's really gonna happen!" It's like money in the bank. I got an email from a man named Jeff Kreines who said he was working on just such a camera. That turned out to be the Kinetta. A year later the Kinetta had a great looking mock-up, a website and a lot of promise. A few more years and there was no camera. Then there was a similar camera called the Drake. More promise, another nice website, but still no camera.

"Then a rumour surfaced about another new camera, this one was called The RED. It was everything my dreamcam would be and possibly more. Compression codecs were getting smarter and better. RED proposed recording an image 4 times the size of HD onto a hard drive.

"If there were Doubting Thomases whirling dervishly just on the mere concept of such a camera, well, when someone claimed they were actually going to produce one they were stirred into a frenzy. Scam! Impossible! Not at that price! Blah, blah, blah...

"Like I said before, when the dreamkillers pull out their knives, expect to see the dream come true. Duck!

"One reason is that the guy behind RED was Jim Jannard. Jannard started Oakley, the maker of high tech sporty sunglasses. I did a little research on him; he also started a funny car drag racing team that wasn't just winning 1/4 mile heats, it was winning championships. Then there was the business stuff, including a story about him coming out with a line of tennis shoes. That didn't work out, and Oakley stock plummeted. So he buys up some stock, moves production overseas, cost drops, profits emerge, the stock triples and the rich get richer. I saw something about his character that doesn't give up, never quits. And if he wants to make a digital 4k handheld camera for $17.5k he's gonna do it even if it ends up costing him a few hundred grand a piece. His pride won't let him fail. In fact, the only way he could fail is if he ran out of money (and since Oakley sold for 2.1 billion, that ain't gonna happen).

The usual suspects gather to get thier greasy fingerprints all over Dale's new RED camera. Left to Right Dale Launer, Ted Schilowitz (RED), Michael Bravin (BandPro) and James Mathers.

"They announced plans to show a mock-up at NAB. I couldn't wait to see it. And there is was, in a glass booth, with a Cooke prime lens literally sagging off one end of it. Which of course made some people suggest it was, well, "like" a scam. Right. Like a billionaire is going to come to NAB to scam some film-makers for a few million dollars? There are easier ways to make a million. So I ponied up a couple grand in deposits and ordered two. After NAB was over, the Doubting Thomases were really screaming. Man, this is a good sign. So I ordered three more. I asked them if I could buy 100, but I never heard back. Eighteen months go by and I show up at RED central in Forest Hills and take home two RED 1 cameras out of the very first batch of cameras ever delivered. Nice. I always thought they would come, I just didn't know when. But now that I have them sitting there, staring at me, begging to be used, I'm feverishly finishing up a script. It's great to have dreams and even greater to see them real-ized, be it a movie, or the camera to make that movie." ~ Dale Launer

As this book goes to press I'm directing the first motion picture to use the RED camera on a Hollywood studio lot. My good friend Joe Di Gennaro is my DP and we are shooting on nearly every location on the Universal back-lot that Steven Spielberg hasn't wrapped up filming "Indiana Jones and the Kingdom of the Crystal Skull."

We're shooting 4K to the diminutive RED-FLASH and downloading to a MacPro station where we pull keys and create rough comps. Once we've got all our elements checked and approved, we move on to the next location.

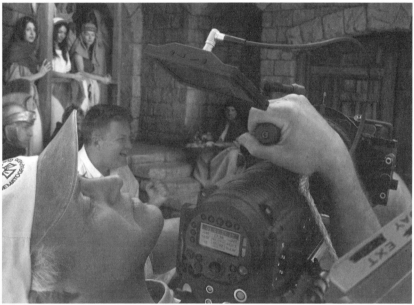

Joe pulls the trigger on Dale's RED camera #24 as the author yells "Action". Fans of the first Pirates of the Caribbean movie will no doubt recognise the set.

Joe's take on it all: *"Although intrigued, I was a bit cautious about relying on such new technology to shoot a feature. The RED had only been released a few weeks before, and I had not had an opportunity to do any testing with it. Fortunatly Scott had been following its development quite closely and had already run it through a series of tests, so I knew that it would work.*

"Initially, I was struck by its size and weight. Although compact, It did not have the lightweight feel of a "handi-cam" (I like a camera to have a bit of mass.. it makes hand-held photography a lot smoother), and I was impressed by the use of 19 mm rods both above and below the camera body, allowing accessories to be attached in a number of different configurations.

"The true proof however, was not the outward appearance, but the internal performance.

"Knowing that we were to shoot the majority of the movie as exteriors, I set up a gray scale in harsh, direct sunlight. and proceeded to run a battery of tests, bracketing exposure both above and below normal, in every different Exposure Index on the menu.

"I knew from past experience with other RAW data systems that, with the exception of the iris and the shutter, most of the settings in the menu do not alter the original material. Color Temperature settings are only metadata for later color correction and Exposure Index adjustments merely set the target for mid-tone exposure in the dynamic range.

"I was impressed by the results. I took the test material to Scott and he bent and stretched the pixels. Neither of us could find complaint about the image quality. Minky was especially pleased with the green-screen sample samples.

(Author's note: We've now pulled a hudred or so greenscreen mattes from that shoot. Minky and I both agree that these are the cleanest mattes we've ever seen.)

"It is obvious that the form/function features of this camera are sill undergoing refinement at this time. However, even with limitations like an as yet incomplete viewing system and slightly obnoxious "hair trigger" buttons and switches, the RED camera behaved admirably on set. Any trepidation I had felt initially was gone by lunchtime on Day One

"We shot in a variety of configurations, from hand-held to Jib flying; shooting from early morning to sunset. The camera held up during both the midday heat and the chilly evening air, in very dusty conditions.

"Tapeless workflow has proven itself to be a reliable and efficient way to take advantage of high resolution image capture, The RED camera uses this technology to fine result; recording data onto compact flash cards, each with a four minute capacity.

"Some may argue that a larger data capacity would be preferable. I am certain that developments are being made to accommodate those desires, however, let me make a case for keeping the on-board recording capacity less than twenty minutes:

"Since the data is being recorded as discrete files, the easiest way to track the file-names is to number the volume (in this case the CF card), and use that as the search reference. Having one enormous bin full of countless takes is a lot harder to keep organized in post production. Also, a large capacity data card puts more of your project at risk. If a card gets lost, damaged or accidentally re-formatted, it is far less devastating to re-shoot ten minutes of material instead of ten hours worth.

"Overall, RED proved itself to be a great imaging tool that lives up to the promises made by its developers. There are refinements still needed, but I can see that those developments will be forthcoming. ~   Joe Di Gennaro

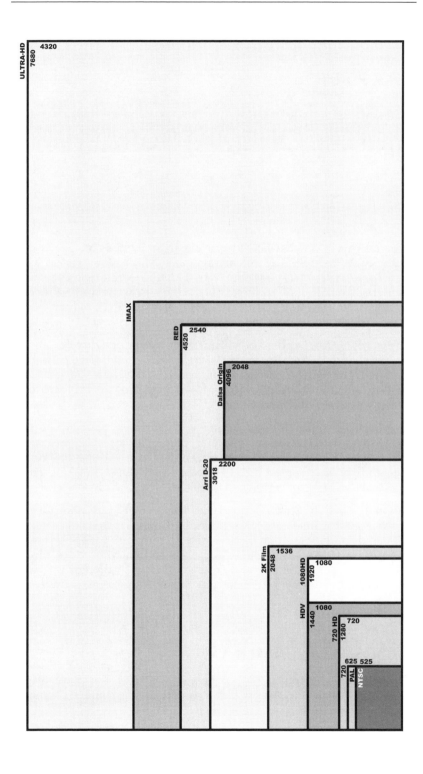

CHAPTER 6

DIGITAL CINEMATOGRAPHY

I started my somewhat eclectic career in cinema as an assistant to Academy Award-winning cinematographer James Wong Howe (*Hud, Rose Tattoo, The Molly Maguires*). Mr. Howe's acerbic wit and rough mannerisms made him an interesting person to work for. He died in the middle of shooting *Funny Lady* with Barbara Streisand and James Caan (talk about lighting the difficult two-shot).

Before his death I often took him to an acupuncturist out in the San Fernando Valley. As we were sitting there one day waiting for his appointment, the chiropractor from the adjoining office came bursting into the waiting room with a gurney full of what was then state-of-the-art video equipment.

He proceeded to play his grainy, jittery, B&W home video for us until Mr. Howe turned to me and asked. *"Scotty, you know why video always looks so crappy?"* I proceeded to ramble on about resolution and sample rates until he interrupted me. *"Video"* he said, *"always looks so crappy cause there's so many crappy people shooting it."* May he rest in peace.

Although harsh, he was actually somewhat correct in his observations. The most unfortunate aspect of digital cinematography is that it generally ends up looking like home video. If you don't particularly want your project to end up looking *"crappy,"* then treat your video camera as if it were a film camera and treat your shots as though you were acquiring something very precious on something very expensive.

CHOOSING A CAMERA

If you haven't figured it out by now, the underlying them of this book is: *Automatic Anything Is Bad*. It is perhaps the single outstanding feature that delineates between *"crappy"* and good.

First thing you need to look for in the selection of an appropriate digital video camcorder is whether or not you can override the automatic functions. Auto-focus, auto-iris, auto-white balance: these functions are created for amateur home videoists, not digital moviemakers.

This is simple; at least it should be. Pick an exposure that gives you a nice depth of field and then turn off your auto exposure and tape your exposure ring in place. If you need more light — bring in the equipment. You need less light, learn how to cut (reduce) the light. Cinematography is all about controlling light physically, not automatically.

If you can't override the auto functions of your camera, stop here, put the book down and go do something else because anything you shoot is going to look bad and drag us all down.

The unmistakable shift as the auto-focus searches for something to lock onto, or the nauseating displacement in depth of field as the auto-iris corrects for changes in brightness or the subtle shift in color-space as the auto-white balance rolls your pallet with every camera move: these are all unmistakable signatures of cheap video and lazy people. They boldly announce that whatever follows should not be taken seriously.

THE LOOK

During the filming of *Mulholland Drive*, David Lynch was looking for a small form factor digital camera to experiment with. I recommended the Sony PD-150 because of its image quality and versatility.

Since the MiniDV and HDV formats have less data than professional systems, the image has a tendency to fall apart much sooner in post.

By timing your look into the camera, and then religiously maintaining that look through your production, you theoretically won't need to further degrade the diminutive format's image any further in post.

A few months after wrapping production on *Mulholland Drive*, we were prepping for the worldwide inaugural commercial for the Sony PlayStation2.

The author pulls the trigger under the direction of David Lynch.

It was a huge project and David says that he's so happy with the look that he's getting from the PD-150 that he wants me to shoot the commercial with it.

David's view of the emerging digital toolset takes a uniquely artistic view. *"It doesn't really matter what way you work, or what medium you work in, it's all about ideas. Every story, every idea wants to be told a certain way. Now, with digital cameras, the really great thing about them is the amount of control you have afterwards to fiddle around and start experimenting and get even more ideas."* ~ David Lynch

DYNAMIC MOTION

Film cameras are generally bulky, heavy affairs. When they move, it is generally with a plodding massiveness that belies their inertia. Video camcorders on the other hand are light, flimsy affairs that we can fling around with mindless abandon.

Go rent your top ten favorite movies, brew a big pot of coffee and get yourself a yellow pad. Now, watch all ten movies and make note of every time the camera flits around or makes any movement that could in any way be construed as coming from an object weighing in at under thirty pounds.

Lightweight camcorders were designed for home video use. If you want your image to move like it came from a film camera, create an environment that causes your tiny camcorder to move like a real film camera. If you're going to use a tripod, get a big one with a large fluid head.

For handheld shots, get yourself a ten-pound weight at the local sporting goods store, or better yet get someone to machine something cool for you. Hook it to your flimsy camcorder and leave it there. It will give your shots a more cinematic feel.

"While there are definite benefits to the simplification that digital offers, I think that there still a few critical tools that need to be developed and refined. These small cameras don't move cinematically, they're light and flimsy.

We need a really nice little Steadicam type device and we need to see more tools like the rigs we made for this commercial, little stabilizers, little dollies and cranes to make them real smooth and cinematic. Then there's the obvious tools that filmmakers need like follow focus, and more mechanical interaction."

In the five years since David Lynch made those observations, the industry has turned on its heel and accommodated.

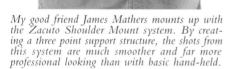

The ever-increasing resolution of small cameras continues to increase as their price and size decrease.

The recent NAB (National Association of Broadcasters) convention in Las Vegas was a testament to the impact that Moore's Law has had on the form factor of digital acquisition.

As the third edition of this book goes to press, manufacturers are introducing very inexpensive, single-chip cameras that generate progressive 1080 HD signals that rival or surpass $100,000 systems that were around when the last edition went to press.

As cameras become smaller it becomes even more important to create stabilizers and movement systems that are designed to give the optimum inertial feel.

My good friend James Mathers mounts up with the Zacuto Shoulder Mount system. By creating a three point support structure, the shots from this system are much smoother and far more professional looking than with basic hand-held.

What is this feel that seems to be so esoteric?

It took me a while to figure it out but after using a number of lighter cameras including the Sony F-950 remote head, the SiliconImaging Mini the Iconix and the Canon HV20, it finally dawned on me.

The perfect dynamic movement for a POV camera is based on the inertia of a twelve-pound object, because that is the weight of an average human head.

An adult human cadaver head, cut off at the C3 vertebra weighs around 5 kg, which is around 8% of the whole body mass.

Since the camera represents the viewer, it makes sense that it should move with the same Newtonian inertia as the human noggin. This is something that can be factored into nearly every POV shot.

MOVEMENT AND BLOCKING

Since camera movement and blocking go hand-in-hand, it is critically important for the director, the DP, and the script supervisor to have a common understanding of the basic tenants of both.

The script super is essentially the director's brain and it is their job to make sure the scene gets shot out in a dynamic but editable progression.

When the director, DP and script super all speak the same lingo and have the same mental shot and blocking references, a production can run noticeably smoother and more efficiently. Camera set-ups are easily the most time-consuming portion of the day.

When everyone speaks the same lingo, and has the same set of mental images, you can easily cut this time down by half. Just think of the impact that would have on your budget.

This is precisely why nearly all successful directors use the same crews over and over. It isn't necessarily that they are the best crew available but rather that they have developed a mental shorthand from sharing a common set of experiences.

When the director turns and says to feature some element or prop, or that he wants a little tension-and-release on the principal, or that he wants a two-shot hand-off on the resolve, the DP should instinctively know what kind of move and feel the director is looking for.

The script super will generally confirm the blocking so the three can agree on camera action (the direction the actors are looking and moving) that will cut with the other shots. *Being on the same page* is much more than a cliché when you're on the set with impatient actors.

This topic alone could easily fill a book and it is strange that more isn't done to make emerging moviemakers aware of what could easily be the single most essential component of both quality and efficiency.

This is the point at which inexpensive, consumer-grade cameras are most valuable. They allow you to get a small crew together and make a movie very cheaply. As I've said before, the true equity isn't in the actual movie, but in the experience.

The first two movies you make will most likely suck in every respect, while the next few movies you make will very often define your craft and style for the rest of your career.

The question is, how do you hit the ground running? What resources are there to help you develop common dialogue, a common set of experiences that won't take years to develop?

The only way I know of to short-cut the process and quickly build a common understanding of camera motion and blocking fundamentals is a DVD series that was created by Per Holmes. Per calls his resource the *Hollywood Camera-Work Master Course,* and it is a most excellent, cinema-grade reference.

I used it just recently as a quick reference to get a director that I haven't worked with before on the same page. Although both of us would be considered veteran filmmakers, a quick review of a couple clips of compound moves from Per's resource solidified his vision in both our minds. The series is also an invaluable resource when dealing with producers and ad agencies as a way to get them to commit to a common vision.

I recommend the series almost daily to new filmmakers as a way to jump-start their learning process. In addition to laying out the basic groundwork of cinematic construction, it also illustrates the various shots and camera moves that can enhance the perceived production value.

"Blocking often grabs so much of our attention that we're forced to choose between doing camera work or nurturing great performances. If we choose acting, the camera work suffers. If we choose camera work, the actors are often left to direct themselves. One of the key goals of the course is to have great camera work become so automatic that we can do both at the same time." ~ Per Holmes

There are a number of free QuickTime samples, scripts and blocking diagrams on his site at: *www.hollywoodcamerawork.us/index.html*

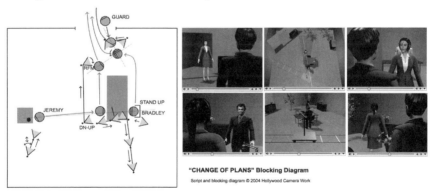

"CHANGE OF PLANS" Blocking Diagram
Script and blocking diagram © 2004 Hollywood Camera Work

For those preparing to embark on their next project, I urge you to download them and view them together with your production team. Then rent, buy or build yourself a jib and try a few of the moves.

Figure out some shots from Per's clips that work for a scene and shoot a page of your script. Don't stress about getting actors or lights, just use any little camera you can get your hands on and see how much faster you work when you're all using the same vocabulary and mental image set.

I'm such a big fan of the series that Per has offered a 30% scholastic discount to readers of this book. Simply type "pixelmonger" into the *School Account Number* field on the third check-out page. And don't forget to drop him a note when you've finished your movie to let him know how much it helped. He loves that stuff.

CAMERA PLACEMENT AND MOVEMENT

Just because you see life at eye-level, don't confine the camera there. In addition to being boring, eye level shots make your movie feel like a documentary. Movies are not life, but rather a synthetically manufactured, alternate reality that hopefully contains all the elements that your audience's lives don't.

The placement of the camera is one of the most important acts in movie making. It is your statement of what the scene represents and how the audience is supposed to view this particular situation.

Camera placement tells your audience how they're supposed to feel about a particular action or character. An ECU (Extreme Close Up) gets us in close to see the subtle play of emotion and perhaps a bit of subtext. A high shot establishes and gives the scene context while a low shot gives a sense of power and control.

During the production of *Citizen Kane*, Orson Welles wanted a low shot looking up at actor Joseph Cotten. He had such a clear understanding of the power of camera placement that he had them jackhammer a hole in the studio floor to put the camera in.

I've always wondered why he didn't just shoot off of a mirror lying on the floor and then flop the shot as an optical, but then, I guess the story about jackhammering the studio floor is much more interesting.

Just as the SteadiCam dramatically opened up the sense of presence for conventional movie makers, a new generation of *motion engineering* devices continue to emerge.

From those little custom devices in the tiny ads in the back of your favorite industry rag to the new generation of body mounted stabilizers, the tools to get an engaging shot are there. All you've got to do is use them.

In the caveman comedy *Homo Erectus*, we used more than 20 different systems to move the camera and establish unique points of view.

For a chase scene that followed Carol Alt running through underground caverns we used the ever-popular Steadicam to generate suspense and enhance the claustrophobic tension of the tight corridors.

We used the truck-based Titan II for a massive, vertical pull-out as the lead (Adam Rifkin) gets mobbed by a tribe of scantly clad Amazon warriors.

For shots of the tribe as they sat and talked around various campfire scenes we used a number of different track-and-dolly sets which added dimension and scope to an otherwise static block.

The author and his 1st AC go "up" for a unique POV atop the mighty Titan II crane.

The ubiquitous Port-A-Jib.

On a particularly remote location we carried in and assembled a 30-foot Lenny crane to get a day's worth of unique shots of the cavemen and their camp.

One such shot followed the trajectory of a CG bug as it flew through the upper branches of a tree down to the camp site where it interacted with numerous actors and finally gets stabbed and eaten by David Carradine.

The ATV Cam and the "Strapped-in-the-back-of-a-pick-up-truck" Cam are time-tested favorites.

We used the diminutive Port-A-Jib on a shot where Tom Arnold's character needed to walk out of a low-wide two-shot and into an eye-line tight for an intimate character reveal.

In a shot where Gary Busey's character leads a charge into battle, the "A" camera operator Sean Fairburn, strapped himself into the back of a pickup for the high-angle shot while your's truly used a custom bungie-mount rigged into the back of an ATV captured the low angle.

The author goes for a ride atop the tiny PD1 dolly.

To create an intimate beauty shot of our female lead (Ali Larter) we lugged the ultra-light Micro-dolly jib into the unusually remote location where it allowed us to skim the camera over the water and then jib up to the magic-hour shot of a very beautiful face.

In a series of shots that took place a half mile under ground, the diminutive PD1 dolly came in handy where the only way to get it in was on the backs of my burly grips.

From the back of ATVs to hanging from ropes dangling over a cliff to the rung of a chopper flying ten feet off the ground, camera movement was essential to keeping the audience engaged.

The Lenny goes together on a remote location.

A good rule of thumb is to keep the camera moving as much as possible. This doesn't mean random movement, but rather movement that enhances the intent of the script.

In addition to simply making a shot more interesting, movement adds dimension and tells the audience more about what is going on.

Movement also gives the audience a clue as to how they should feel. As much as we all love bold dynamic moves, it is the little moves that really embellish the narrative.

As you might imagine, the question that I get ask most often is in regard to what camera to buy. My answer is almost always the same:

"Take the money you were going to spend on a camera and get the cheapest, piece-of-crap camera you can find. Then take the money that you've got left over and buy yourself a good jib."

Cameras come and go. Anything you buy today will be worthless in a year or two, but a jib, now there's a truly great invest-ment.

By owning your own jib you can practice anytime you get an idea. The more you use it, the more unique your shots will become and you'll actually begin to develop your own signature style. 99.9% of people with new cameras simply shoot what they see. Where's the style? Where's the craft?

Intel-A-Jib.

It takes time to develop craft, and a lot of trial and error. Simply throw that piece-of-crap camera on your jib arm and shoot away. Try every move you can think of. Download Per's free QuickTime demos and recreate his scenes. I guarantee it will take a lot of really bad shots to get a single truly good take. You don't want to be doing that stuff on set.

I keep an old camera set up on a short arm jib in my office. My walls are full of masks that I collected back in my National Geographic days, and when I'm taking a break or sitting around, I practice moves on'em. Even though my main job isn't that of an operator, CHOPS IS CHOPS.

When people stop by, they invariably gravitate to the camera and do a move or two. Since the video signal of the camera feeds into my production monitor, it makes a great reference when I'm talking shop with other production people.

Some moves build tension while others release it. Some moves are used to establish a shift of emotions or focus while other moves convey hidden agendas and ulterior motives. The way you set and move your camera contributes more to the perceived value of your production than any other single factor with the possible exception of lighting.

JIB-ER-JABBER

How do you know which jib is right for you? While that question is not for me to answer, I will offer up my own personal observations.

Two of the better, all-around, heavy-duty jibs for quick set-up and rugged dependability are the Jimmy-Jib, and the Intel-A-Jib. Sturdy as rocks, just as heavy and at nearly $10K (including the case), expensive as heck.

MicroDolly Jib

If price and weight are no object, either of these are safe bets to put on the gear list.

For a much lighter system with good set-up speed (only a few thousand less), the MicroDolly, Micro-Jib is a great rig. It folds down to a few small soft packs and has more innovative amenities than any jib made. The superb quality of the titanium manufacturing gives you an unusually solid platform with an easy 14-foot extension that weighs in around 30 pounds total. Truly an unparalleled bit of craftsmanship.

Widely considered one of the mainstays of independent production, the Losmandy Porta-Jib costs about half as much as the Jimmy Jib or Intel-A-Jib but doesn't seem to have the stability of either when using extensions. It is also a bit esoteric to build and a notorious finger pincher.

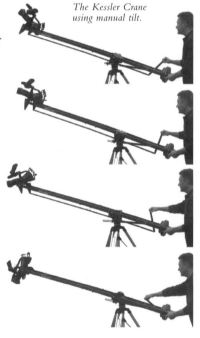

The Kessler Crane using manual tilt.

There are a lot of inexpensive jib arm systems on the market and they will all give you a better shot than simply using your tripod or hand holding your camera.

Which system is right for you? Why not go to a trade show and try them all?

While jibs are justifiably part of the camera department, the director also needs to be cognizant of their potential to help tell the story.

A little time with a jib is a very good investment for visualizing your scenes.

Some jibs and cranes only move the camera vertically and horizontally. They generally maintain the camera at a preset angle which is usually parallel to the floor.

Some jibs have the capacity to tilt the camera, and by rotating the camera's mounting plate 90 degrees, they also allow Dutch, yaw or side tilts.

The addition of a Power-Head allows full axis control at all heights. Remote control heads are especially handy in situations where the camera is inaccessible and an operator-carrying crane is too large or expensive. They can add a level of complexity to shots that if done correctly, add enormous production value.

Master the "Smart End" of the crane before you move to the back.

Some jibs work better when controlled from the rear while others work best when controlled at the camera. Some work better when mounted on dollies and some are better on sticks.

There is no single crane or jib that does everything.

I do a lot of pick-up shots and visual effects elements where I throw my gear in the SUV and head out to the desert or up into the mountains. I want a cost-effective system that is light enough to handle by myself, sturdy enough to stand up to many years of unkind abuse and versatile enough to switch quickly from big extensions to intimate micro-moves.

If I were to recommend a single unit that was cost effective, versatile, easy-to-use, unusually well made and rugged, it is the Kessler Crane.

The Kessler's dual arm construction may seem a little unconventional, but by mounting lower on the tripod head it provides much greater stability in a light-weight form-factor.

The dual arm design also reduces twist, adds strength and easily handles cameras from a fully loaded Arri 535 film camera down to the latest consumer, HDV flavor-of-the-month. It also has the sturdiest arm lock of any system I've tried and the added bonus of being able to tilt the camera using the third axis lever arm has come in very handy on a growing number of shots.

MULTIPLE CAMERAS

Now this might sound a little counter-intuitive but one of the easiest ways to save money is to shoot two cameras. You're thinking. *"But Scott; that's two operators, two rentals, two assistants. How could that possibly save money?"*

The number of pages you get in a day is determined by a very simple formula which includes the amount of time it takes costume, make-up and hair to get your actors ready, the amount of time it takes props and art department to get your set ready and the amount of time it takes you to cover the scene.

There really isn't much you can do about costume, makeup, hair and art. They generally take the same amount of time regardless of how many bodies you throw at them. On set however, two cameras almost double the number of pages you can shoot in a day. While a third camera generally doesn't give

The addition of a second camera can be a big cost-saving decision. Top Gun Sean Fairburn calabrates the F-900's before we head out for a day of shooting.

you an extra page, the added cost of running extra cameras is a lot cheaper than extra days floating all the people in all the departments as well as your cast.

Factor in the rentals, catering, transportation and permits and you'll soon see that the extra pages that multiple cameras can give you are easily the best cost-saving investment there is.

Consider running a three-camera system with your "A" camera oper-ator shooting the money shots. With dramatic scenes, have them shooting the lead actor's face. For battle scenes have them shooting principal stunt action and for comedy, have them shoot the set-ups.

"B" camera is generally less specific and covers the two-shots, general action and the punch lines and reactions. "C" camera is your ace in the hole. I use a lot of film students. USC, UCLA, NYU, UT, they're everywhere. They may not have the chops of a veteran but they tend to know what they don't know.

Students are usually looking for practical expression of the two or four years of book learning and lectures they've endured and they tend to listen to direction. Students also tend to have a good understanding of **... the first take is almost always the one with the magic.** the need for coverage and know it when they see it. More than any other single factor, coverage is what separates amateur from profes-sional productions.

Most directors think in a series of master shots; they just can't help it. The DPs main duty is to represent the audience and actually fight for the time to get multiple angles of the scene and shots that allow them to connect transparently with the characters.

The script super is the conscience of the script and must be comfort-able enough with their capabilities to wrangle both the director and the DP should they feel that a scene wasn't covered adequately or properly.

Coverage generally isn't scripted but it is the·glue that editors use to bind the shots together. In far too many instances, it is the lack of coverage that is most responsible for turning potentially great movies into discount bin mediocrity.

Think of the master shot as a slab of raw meat. A little steak tartar goes a long way. But cut up that meat and throw it in a pot with the "B" camera's vegetables and broth, add some C-cam spice and you've got yourself a meal that is not only more tasty, but far more fulfilling and agreeable to a wider spectrum of palates.

For those who find themselves truly strapped for budget and crew, set one camera on a tripod and hand-hold the other so one's over the shoulder and one's on the face for the close-up. There, you just saved a lot of time and energy. Heck, get three cameras. The more coverage you get now, the more choices you'll have later.

After you develop a rhythm with your actors you'll find that the first take's almost always the one with the magic. Generally you'd shoot a couple more takes then come around for the close-up or the two-shot and then do the series all over again. But chances are, you're not using seasoned actors. They probably don't know how to modulate their performances. They probably don't have the slightest understanding of recreating the same performance you just shot from the side when you come around for the close-up.

Mismatches in the flow of the performance might not look like much on the set, but by the time you get into editing they won't cut. Even if you do recognize the problem, the more you shoot, the more it'll just keep getting muddier and muddier and you'll never get back the magic of that first take.

In conventional film production the whole process is so convoluted with DPs and their crews loading, cleaning, checking, and logging each shot that hardly anyone ever uses multiple cameras. But hey, you're not using film. Cheapest thing you've got is videotape. Burn it up baby!

Aside from the obvious cost savings, the actors knows that several angles are being shot at once so they might want to put more effort into the portrayal.

And while we're on the topic of burning video, don't be foolish enough to try to save money by not running the tape a bit before and after takes. Heads and tails are very important. Just because you pressed the little red button doesn't mean that you're recording. Do it like the pros and let the tape get up to speed. Sure video starts up a lot faster than film but its always better to have a little extra than not enough.

DIGITAL PUBERTY

Having been fortunate enough to work with a number of consummate filmmakers, the single unifying factor in their methodology seems to be that they are driven by a need to engage the audience. The more resolution you throw up on the screen, the easier it is for your audience to become involved in your vision.

Higher resolution is the hallmark of professionalism. Projecting something shot on miniDV to an audience that is expecting cinematic quality is a potentially carrier-ending faux pas for anyone who doesn't have the resumé to back it up.

At some point in your career, you will cease to be a digital movie maker and just be a moviemaker. The change is something that will sneak up on you and change your view of the industry and your place in it.

For many, it comes the first time they stand at the back of a theater full of people who paid money to watch their movie. For others, it happens the first time they walk into a Blockbuster and see their movie up on the shelves.

Whenever it hits you, it will feel as though you've just gone through puberty once again. Old habits won't fit the way they did before, as you re-evaluate your motivations.

Hopefully you'll become a defender of the experience where every project you get involved in, every shot you take, is driven by a desire to give the audience an enjoyable and worthwhile two hours.

Let's say that you've already managed to make a couple of shorts, maybe even a passable long-form feature. The fact that you've actually gotten the train to leave the station and brought it back with cast and crew intact qualifies you as a professional.

> **At some point in your career, you will cease to be a digital movie maker and just be a moviemaker.**

Maybe you had a little success at a festival, maybe you didn't — it doesn't really matter. The fact that you actually took a project from concept-to-can is really the only relevant qualifier. Whether or not your movie was any good is not for me to judge.

Since you're now a professional moviemaker, you need to make professional choices. The problem comes when the information you make your decisions on comes from ads and articles rather than experience.

People like myself who write articles for magazines can only get those articles published if they sell something or support the publication's mythos. This isn't a bad thing, its just commerce.

Now obviously there are a lot of magazines that require a lot of articles. The reality is that production people are generally too busy making a living to write articles every month.

We end up with far too many articles written by people who have little to no real world experience and who are simply reformatting a manufacturer's articulate press release.

Please don't misunderstand, there is a lot of misinformation in books as well, but since they aren't driven by advertising, the info is less commercially motivated.

So after shooting many kinds of projects on every flavor of HD, using every camera in this book, here is my very best attempt at the bottom line of HD.

HD FAIRY TALES

MYTH: You need less crew to shoot HD.

FACT: Since cinematic methodology remains the same, the number of crew in every department required to create a comparable level of quality also remains the same. The essential difference is in the camera department where the Film Loader is replaced with an HD Engineer at a pay rate between a Camera Operator and the DP.

MYTH: You need fewer lights to shoot HD.

FACT: If you rate the HD Camera at 320 ASA for best performance, you will need the same number and type of lights as if you were shooting 320 ASA Film.

MYTH: HD is cheaper to shoot than film.

FACT: With shorts, the savings in film and development is generally offset by the added amount of footage that you shoot. Takes tend to go much longer with HD because they can. The benefits in not cutting are generally mirrored in more consistent performances. With features, there is a slight savings, but nothing that should amount to more than 2% of your budget.

MYTH: HD camera packages will be less expensive to rent than film packages.

FACT: Industry writer Glenn Estersohn did research on camera rental prices in New York, Chicago and Los Angeles. He compared un-discounted published *"rate card"* prices and found that the average Sony HDW-F900 rental was 9% more expensive than the average rental for an Aaton 35-3, Arriflex 535B or Golden Panaflex GII, all with color video assist. His findings seem to be holding steady.

MYTH: HD saves an enormous amount of money in post-production.

FACT: This is true. Upwards of 70% in effects-heavy projects. (However, don't forget that these savings can be reduced when it comes to on-line and other post processes, where HD equipment may be relatively scarce and definitely expensive.)

MYTH: HD looks better than film when projected.

FACT: Good HD looks much better than old film. Head-to-head film gives you more latitude while good HD will give your more Colors.

LENSES

Unfortunately there is no such thing as a perfect lens; they all suffer from varying degrees of chromatic aberration, diffraction, slight variances in the index of refraction and low- tolerance manufacturing anomalies.

Generally a glass lens is far superior to a resin one, and a coated lens is always superior to an uncoated one.

The more elements (individual lenses) a system has, the greater the resolving power and accuracy. The essential quality of a lens can be expressed in terms of F-stop or T-factor.

The quality of cinematic lenses like a Zeiss DigiPrime or the always-popular Panavision Primo is far, far, far superior to that of any prosumer camcorder.

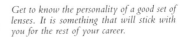

Get to know the personality of a good set of lenses. It is something that will stick with you for the rest of your career.

There is an unsubstantiated rumor that the video camera manufacturers actually de-engineer the camcorder lenses so that they don't compete with their far more expensive ENG (Electronic News Gathering) and broadcast systems.

Comparing them side by side generates a compelling argument for these rumors since the CCDs are often quite similar.

So there you are, starting out with inferior glass, or plastic as the case may be. Compounding the deficiencies in light gathering, focus and image sharpness is the fact that virtually all camcorders come with zoom lenses which further degrades the already insubstantial image quality.

By adapting standard cinematic methodologies to the digital video metaphor we can begin to create an ambiance, if not the actual resolution, of studio-quality fare. By looking at how the camcorder handles light we can work around its limitations and get a step nearer to creating that truly epic film-like look.

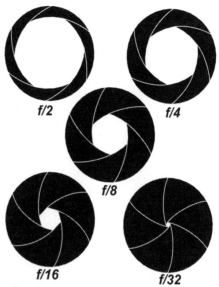

Exposure is the calculation of light intensity over time. Or, Exposure = Intensity x Time. Every increase or decrease in time or intensity will inversely affect the other in equal proportion. If you double the amount of light but decrease the amount of time by half, the exposure remains the same.

The wider the iris, the more light that hits the CCD and the shorter the depth of field becomes.

The aperture controls the amount of light that is allowed to pass through a lens. It is regulated by the iris, which looks and operates similarly to the iris in our own eyes.

When shooting in low light situations the iris opens up to allow more light to fall onto the CCDs. Similarly, a well-lit page of type is far easier to read than a poorly lit one.

The amount of opening of the iris is expressed as an F-stop which is a mathematical equivalent calculated by dividing the focal length by the effective diameter of the lens that is in use at that particular setting.

A lower F-stop opens up the aperture, allowing in more light and shortening the depth of field.

With a wide open aperture an object that is in focus at five feet will have a field of focus extending only a few feet or even inches towards and away from the lens.

As the lens is *stopped down* and the iris is closed tighter, the amount of light hitting the CCDs is greatly reduced and the field of focus is extended.

The same object that is in focus at five feet may have a field of focus that extends from just a few inches in front of the lens on out to infinity.

The vast majority of camcorders don't have F-stop indicators on their lenses, and in most cases attenuate the luminance value of the initial video signal to give an electrically arrived at correlate F-stop value. The F-stop is usually displayed in the viewfinder window next to the shutter speed.

Lighting ratios are what define character in a monocular world and the single best way to determine your ratios is with a light meter. Nothing will give you consistently better composition and exposures. Failing that, you've got to become familiar with the manual control of aperture and shutter speed.

SHUTTER

The other way the lens/camera regulates light is the shutter. Film cameras have a physical shutter that cuts off the flow of light while the next frame of film is dragged forward.

The standard motion picture shutter consists of a spinning disk with an opening of a specified angle that rotates at the frame rate of the film. A shutter that has an opening of 180 would be open half the time.

Since the standard frame rate of cinema is 24 fps and the shutter is open half the time, the shutter speed would be 1/48 of a second. This is often rounded off to 1/50 of a second in many film cameras.

A 90-degree shutter.

Video CCDs, on the other hand generate a steady stream of image/data. Since there are two fields to every frame, and NTSC operates at 30 fps, most NTSC video cameras shoot at a shutter speed of 1/60 second while PAL runs at 25 fps and shoots at 1/50. The baseline objective is to use a shutter speed that is twice as fast as your frame rate.Many HDV cameras are capable of generating a 24 fps sequence but more often than not, use some sort of math to pull the cinematic cadence from the 60Hz or 50Hz time base.

Most quality video cameras have an electronic shutter which will be able to give you shutter speeds from 1/4 second up to 1/10,000 second. Even though the camera is recording at 1/60 or 1/50 of a second, setting the shutter at a lower rate such as 1/15 second, creates a *look* that many people feel echoes the cinematic nuance of film.

I personally find this effect quite disturbing but am putting it out there so that you have it in your quiver. Once you enter the realm of frame rate experimentation, testing becomes imperative.

You can also use the shutter to control the amount of light without changing your F–stop or adding neutral density filters. Each consecutive exposure time is cutting down or increasing the amount of light entering the camera by one F–stop, which means that it is effectively halving or doubling the exposure.

Don't go above 1/250 second without doing some tests to see if you like the strobing effect that it creates. Remember; the object is to find an F–stop that allows you to create depth in your compositions (start with an F/4) and then use that stop to shoot your entire scene.

MATTE BOX

The camera is a system designed to collect and control a stream of reflected light within the limits of its designated recording specifications.

One of the most practical and significant steps towards controlling the light that enters the lens is the matte box light shade.

It serves a dual purpose as its name would suggest of shading the forward lens element from stray shafts of light while also allowing you a mechanism for attaching a variety of filters.

2 Stage Matte Box from Vocas

You'd be hard pressed to find a professional film or video camera that didn't sport one of these most basic tools of the trade.

In many instances, the shade that accompanied your camcorder actually offers superior light shading. It is only when you factor in the copious use of lens filters that the Matte Box changes from the lame affectation that marks posers and gadget freaks to an essential tool for professional production.

The difference lies solely in the use of filters.

A good workable matte box should have at least two filter trays (stages) and one of them should be able to rotate. They should both be lockable as well so that lens movement won't throw your polarizer or gradient filter off axis.

To be effective the matte box should have a shade that can extend at least six inches from the front element and be solid enough so that it doesn't wiggle around. More than one shot has been ruined by a flag or shade slowly creeping into frame.

To make sure the matte box's occlusion is as close to the image edge as possible without impinging, put your finger at the centers of the four sides and move it in toward the center until it shows up in the viewfinder.

Your finger should be just short of the first joint. Any less and you run the chance of the matte box cutting into the image, any more and you won't get the full light-shading benefits.

THE SECRET OF NEUTRAL DENSITY

Since you've now got your trusty matte box hooked up to your camcorder you can easily attach neutral density filters to it. These are plain gray filters that absorb light of all colors in equal amounts. Think of them as sunglasses for your camera. They are used to control the quantity of light that enters the lens, not the quality. You should consider obtaining a small collection of filters before you start shooting.

While you can spend well over a thousand dollars on a really nice glass set of filters, for camcorders with consumer lenses a decent set of cut gelatin filters is often sufficient for a basic introduction. ND 0.1 will allow 80% of the light through which would increase your exposure by 1/3 F-stop. The ND 0.6 reduces transmission by 25%, which is an even two F-stop increase. At the top of the practical collection would be the ND 0.9, which would result in a three F-stop increase, or 87% reduction in the amount of light entering the camera.

What we are trying to do here is stabilize and reduce the low light sensitivity of the camcorder so that it begins to echo the light-handling characteristics of a conventional film camera. By throwing an ND over the lens we are forcing the scene to be lit just the same way you would be forced to light a conventional film set. Once you get your mind around this concept, and accept that it will entail far more work than simply turning on your automatic camcorder and shooting away, you will start to generate some truly cinematic shots.

POLARIZING FILTER

Since light bounces around in all directions along its axis, the reflections that it creates in windows, water and glass lenses often create an impenetrable barrier. A polarizing filter is an essential accessory that can reduce or eliminate these reflections. In exterior shots it can darken the sky and create more dramatic clouds.

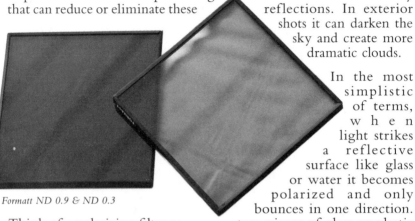

In the most simplistic of terms, when light strikes a reflective surface like glass or water it becomes polarized and only bounces in one direction.

Formatt ND 0.9 & ND 0.3

Think of a polarizing filter as two pieces of glass or plastic with some microscopic venetian blinds laminated in between. What these micro-blinds do is essentially filter out all of the random light and allow only the parallel-polarized light to pass.

The object is not to eliminate all of the reflection but rather to reduce it to a point where it becomes a suggestion of reflectivity.

Polarizing filters are also used for penetrating haze and in many cases make a good ND filter. While not as constant as a conventional ND, a good polarizer is generally good for a filter factor of ND 0.2 or 1 1/2 F-stops.

When shooting trees and foliage a polarizing filter can raise the color saturation of leaves and shiny surfaces significantly by reducing their surface specularity.

MORE FILTER HACKS

More than any other factor, latitude is the principal shortcoming of digital acquisition.

There are a number of hacks that can help you stretch your latitude, top of which is to use grad filters. By sliding a gradient into your matte box so that the edge of the grad is parallel to the horizon, you drastically cut down the relative brightness of the sky and effectively increase your dynamic range.

If you need to shoot someone in that same frame, bounce some fill onto the part of them that is darkened by the filter. Your bounce will have no effect on your background.

There are also a number of variations of low con filters but you need to make sure that they are a quality product or it will eat into your colorspace considerably.

Nothing adds a little qualitative nuance to your image like a little black or white *mist* filter. A long-time secret ingredient of high-end videographers and cinematographers, the pro-mist adds a tiny bit of halation to the image which has the perceived effect of softening the minute imperfections in the human face.

For veteran actresses try using the Formatt Ultra-Gold mist in varying densities.

I use the Formatt line of filters almost exclusively and have quite a collection of them. They have a terrific range of colors and styles as well as some of the best fall-off ratios on their gradients.

Unique to the Formatts is the metal edge that prevents glass from nicking and also keeps the

The Formatt ND 0.6 Grad held up to the horizon line. Note how the sky is knocked down but the houses hold their exposure.

grease from my lunch burrito from seeping in between the glass covering and damaging the actual filter gel.

HOME-MADE FILTERS

One of the nicest establishments is the sun rising or setting over your location, but you very rarely see it done well. The trick is to build a big gradient filter and hook it to a clock motor or some sort of very slow, very even movement source. As the sun comes up, gradually slide the darker portion of your filter over the lens.

There are a number of good materials you can use to make filters. Keep in mind that any minor abnormalities will generally be out of your field of focus, so density and color are the main factors here. Grab a nice piece of clear plastic (12" x 24") at the hardware store and dip it repeatedly into hot (almost boiling) Rit dye.

A strong combination of black and dark blue is really great for general use. More variance in the dipping gives you a more gradual gradation.

This is an ion transfer methodology that is very similar to how very expensive filters are made. You're not really interested in coating the piece of plastic as you are in working the molecules of dye into those of the plastic.

After every six or eight dips you should wipe the surface of the plastic to eliminate schmutz and globs of junk that are left over from the spaghetti sauce that the pot was last used for.

When you're done, take good care of your custom filter, as you'll probably end up using it now and then for the rest of your life. Mine is almost 20 years old.

Just recently we needed to pan from an assassin who was hiding in a cave to a man on horseback in open sun. By mounting the filter plate sideways and panning through the gradation we were able to hold the densities without the addition of location lighting.

The home-made filter plate was also used in an extreme high-altitude, mountaineering environment where the contrast ratio between snow and sky was quite literally off the charts.

The filter was mounted to a couple tent poles that were stuck in the ice, and then aligned with the dense side down and the grad just at the junction between sky and snow. It not only dropped the contrast ratio nearly four stops but since it was mounted in a fixed position the camera could pan and tilt within the dimensions of the filter plate while holding exposure..

This should go without saying: *"no automatic anything!"*

SUN/MOON CUTTER

Tired of having a nice composition with a blown-out sun or moon in the background? Same principle, same pot of boiling Rit dye. This time you use a cotton swab to dye a single spot in the upper center of your piece of plastic.

The object is to keep at it until you've got a nice dark splotch about the size of an M&M. Don't stress about streaks or small irregularities, as your depth of field will obfuscate them. Unlike the straight gradient where you mount it to the pan collar of your fluid head, the spot filter is fixed. Since it doesn't move with the camera, you might want to consider using a larger piece of plastic.

NIX THE ZOOM

One of the biggest tip-offs that you're watching video is a zoom. DON'T ZOOM! DON'T EVER ZOOM! It doesn't matter whether or not you think a zoom will enhance the end result, you are wrong!

Watch your ten favorite movies. You can use that same yellow pad again and make a note each time you see a zoom: not a *dolly* or a *truck* or a *push* where the camera actually moves closer to the subject; I'm talking zoom. After viewing all ten of your favorite movies please notice how nice and clean your yellow pad still is.

With the rare exception of specialty moves, like Robert Burks' inventive push-and-zoom effect in Alfred Hitchcock's *Vertigo*, the zoom is the truest mark of a videographer. Zooms are for sports, weddings and home video. Filmmakers on the other hand, generally use a very expensive set of *prime* lenses or at least the metaphor.

A *prime* is a lens of fixed focal length. In DP lingo it refers to the distance between the optical center of the lens and the film plane, when the lens is focused at infinity (endless point in space, not the car). To the videographer it means that you frame the shot using the zoom function selecting a setting between *wide* and *telephoto* and then leave it there as you make your shot.

If you need to get the actor's face to fill the scene, get up off your ass and physically move closer. The object is to move the camera. A camera move gives a scene dynamics and a greater sense of presence. It helps develop a point of view and establishes the environment in which you're telling the story. Yes there are professional zoom lenses but they are generally used as a rapidly accessible set of prime focal lengths.

I've gotten a lot of flack from that statement; all of it from people who have never created a single thing of value. Laziness is perhaps the single greatest barrier to success in any endeavor and as any good ad person can attest to, you can't go far wrong pandering to the seven deadly sins. Don't zoom.

THE JIM VARNEY EFFECT

The tendency with small video camcorders is to get too close to the subject. They're small and unobtrusive, almost ubiquitous in contemporary society.

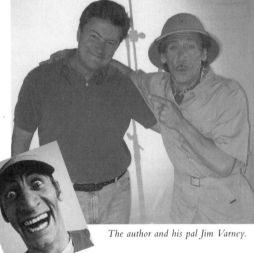

Add to this the high number of people who are using a camera-mounted microphone and its probably safe to say that this is one of the bigger factors in the *video* look.

The problem with shooting someone from a short distance is that you'll generally need to use a rather wide lens that has an angle of view in excess of 90 degrees. People tend to look goofy when shot with wide-angle *short* lenses.

The author and his pal Jim Varney.

I call it the *Jim Varney Effect*, and while the late comedian made a career out of it, the look leaves a bit to be desired on your leading lady.

A lens that has an angle of view in the 10-degree range will generally put you at least 12 feet away from the subject annd will generally give you a far better sense of the person's character. Test this as often as it takes till you get the feel.

THE SWEET SPOT

You've got to experiment with your system to find its particular sweet spot. Short of buying a light meter, you'll need to buy build or steal some test charts. You'll need these for the rest of your illustrious career so plan on spending a little time and money on getting something that works for you.

Go outside on a bright sunny day and shoot a few seconds of a person standing in full sunlight utilizing all of the automatic functions of your spiffy new camcorder. Next, set up the 85% gray card in the same location and angle it so that sunlight is falling fully upon it. Now, turn off the auto functions of your camcorder.

You will probably need to read the instruction manual of your particular camcorder to see how to override the auto-iris and auto-focus functions. The F-stop equivalent on camcorders is generally displayed in a small LCD window within the viewfinder and has a tiny button or dial for adjustment.

The idea is to place various densities of ND filters over your lens until you arrive at a good average setting to use to shoot your entire production. F4 is a nice place to start for masters because it gives you a nice depth of field, not too deep, not too shallow, and it is just shy of the middle of any professional lens, which gives you plenty of room to move.

For tight shots or a nice intimate two-shot, an F2.4 throws the background out a bit more and gives a nice isolating effect to the actor's dialogue. Using combinations of the ND 0.2 will also match the transmission index of most polarizing filters and allow you to regulate your exposure while maintaining your F-stop.

Once you're locked in to a nice solid F4, have someone step in front of your gray card. With the auto-focus feature on your camcorder disabled, perform a manual focus using the highlight in their eye as a point of focus. It is often helpful to zoom into the eye, focus and then zoom back out and re-frame the shot. This is the only time that you're allowed to use the zoom!

The sharpest setting for most lenses is generally 1 1/2 to 2 stops down from the widest aperture while the sharpest resolved image is obtained with the greatest depth of field using the smallest aperture. The method we're working with here should give us the best of both worlds.

Once you've got a good recording of your subject in full light, rig a white bed sheet, or better yet a section of a white army surplus parachute above them so that the sunlight is diffused, Shoot a few seconds more of your subject.

Next get a bright white surface at least several feet square and position it to the side and slightly below the eye line of your subject. Make sure the surface is bouncing light back toward the subject's face.

Record a few seconds of this. As simplistic as this exercise sounds, when you view the resulting images on a video monitor you should notice a far more crafted look in the later shots than in your original one.

Unless you're shooting a documentary you shouldn't obsess about shooting the reality of the scene. You're telling a story and manipulating the viewer's perceptions. Take liberties with reality if it helps you convey the mood or intent of the scene — it's your tale to tell.

VANILLAFICATION

Talking about lighting is like talking about religion. In my religion, light exists as a three-dimensional volume. It falls off at a square of the distance and interacts with surfaces to generate secondary and tertiary volumes as well.

A meter tells me quantitatively what my lighting ratios are in a three-space, a waveform tells me the 2D results and a monitor gives me a visual reference that can be used to judge the picture qualitatively. Nothing gets replaced, nothing is better or worse than. Different tools do different things. Cinematography is a craft, and every bit of gizmology that negates understanding contributes a vanillifying effect to the cinematic future of digital acquisition.

Down in the basement studio of The Academy of Motion Picture Arts and Sciences, Germano Saracco, David Stump, Jonathan Erland (lower center), the author and Lou Levinson all try to agree on how to light the most famous chart in the world. http://www.oscars.org/council/advanced.html

You will know that you are becoming a professional when you find yourself resenting the atomization of the cinematic process.

A lot of folks here in Hollywood work in the sitcom world where you throw up a coop the size of a school bus and fill everything with a baseline ambiance. It is a look that makes a lot of people a lot of money. I imagine a monitor is indispensable in those situations. Lots of producers, lots of opinions. It's all good.

Then there's drama. Unlike the knee-jerk simplicity of sitcoms, drama is more about evoking empathy. It is about performance and the subtle play of emotion across the human face.

It is more about gray scale and luminance value than it is about color. A good one stop of falloff across the face is a good place to start for anything tighter than a cowboy closeup (top of the hat to bottom of the gun).

Light meters establish a quantifiable value that can factored into the decision-making process. Among other significant factors, they allow you to match ratios on a million dollar face while doing pick-ups a week later. Monitors are good to share the wealth and arrive at consensus, but then that's a different methodology, a different religion.

You rarely see a great cinematographer pulling out his light meter but that's because they've developed such a fine sense that they can actually see light. They hold up their hand and they know what the value is.

Great cinematographers don't use meters because they don't believe in them; they don't use meters because they are one.

So that's my say on meters. Its one of the pieces that keeps HD from becoming auto-everything mediocrity. A monitor is a good way to judge what your final shot is going to look like on a monitor. No doubt about it.

CHARTS

Professionals DPs and camera operators all have their favorite charts. For the vast majority of production people the DSC series has been a world standard since its inception in 1967.

As a big fan of the DSC series, I rarely if ever start a shoot without one and on numerous occasions have worked on productions where several people all have their favorite DSC chart with them.

My personal collection includes the versital CamBook, the essential MultiBurst and of course the CamAlign. Like most people who use charts on a daily basis, I generally customize them by adding a few bits that are specific to that project.

Most people who shoot visual effects add some ChromaKey tape to the corners of their charts while several prominent DPs add specific skin tone chips that are in the same palette as the lead actors.

My friend Tim Sassoon does a lot of large-format VFX work and likes to have some highly saturated chroma strips on his chart. Another good friend, Pierre de Lispionois, does a lot of plate work for his ultra-high-end CG characters to roam around in. He likes to have a globe or ball near the chart that let's his graphic artists know where the light is coming from.

There are a lot of different people in the production chain and each one is looking for a different bit of information from the chart.

- The 1st AC wants to check the back-focus.

- Engineering wants to set levels.

- The operator wants to make sure that they're not crushing or blowing out.

- The gaffer wants to see the grayscale.

- The DP wants to see if the skin tones are all going to match.

- The DI people want full spectrum reference to match sequences.

- The colorists want a standardized color reference.

- The graphics folks are dying to know what the key ratios were.

- The compositors want to know what the angle of view was.

- The 3D geeks want to know the lighting setup and lens info.

- The Post Super wants to know of colorspace and image hits.

- The editors want density and color reference between shots.

A shooter's chart for a guy like me is entirely different than an engineering chart like the 28R-SL, so when DSC's David Corley ask for my two cents, he got more than he bargained for.

Since a majority of the movies and shows I shoot have some sort of visual effects in them, it seemed sensible to design a chart specifically to meet the needs of this segment of the industry.

www.dsclabs.com/vfx_visual_effects.htm

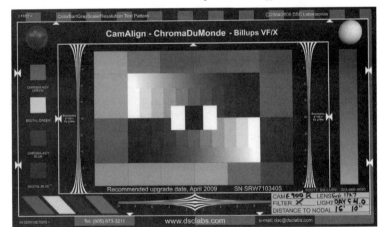

I wanted to call it "THE FIRST CHART WITH BALLS" *but DSC Labs insisted on calling it the* "BILLUPS VFX."

Among the 36 diagnostic features of the chart are the grayscale and sky-blue ramp. These help identify banding introduced in image processing due to filters and applications that reduce color-space.

Digital Green and Blue paint chips from Composite Components plus Rosco's Chroma Key Green and Blue are a big help in calibrating between the key and fill when doing green screen work.

High Chroma slashes are very useful for checking and tracking chroma aliasing through post. The chart's black background provides cleaner histograms and crisper feedback using desktop diagnostics.

There are inch and centimeter scales top and bottom which allow you to easily compute the angle of view by knowing the chart's distance to camera. This and other pertinent camera info is included on the dry-erase data information panel in the lower right corner.

Additionally, there are two hemispherical reflectance spheres. The black sphere not only shows the number, position and type of lighting (spot or flood), but also the hue or color filtration of individual lights. The white sphere shows the integrated level and color temperature.

As with a number of tools I've developed or consult on, I don't receive any sort of financial income or reimbursement from their sale. I sold all rights to my chart design to the Canadian based DSC Labs for a *Looney*, which is a Canadian silver dollar.

GAIN

Most cameras have a gain switch that increases the camera's sensitivity in low-light situations. When you increase the gain, you add noise to the image, which in some instances looks a bit like the grain found in a fast film emulsion. Many people use the gain setting as a short cut to lighting. Don't!

True, a little noise is the fastest way to add a cinematic nuance to your video image but there are far better ways to do this in post.

What you lose by boosting gain in the acquisition stage is the ability to control the amount of grain you end up with in your final print.

What might seem like teeny-tiny little specks of grain on your video monitor will look like a full-on blizzard when projected. Once its in your image, it's almost impossible to get out.

A drop of super glue is the best thing you can do to your gain switch.

VIDEO LEVELS

On the other end of the scale is the problem of too much light. When shooting video that will later be printed to film you should avoid shooting in direct sunlight whenever possible. The contrast ratio generated by direct sunlight is far greater than video cameras can handle and the resulting image problems are only worsened in the printing process.

Most professional video cameras have a mechanism known as the zebra indicator which lets the operator know if there are areas of illumination within the scene that exceed the camera's ability to record it.

Wherever the brightness exceeds the pre-set level, the zebra indicator superimposes a striped pattern over the area. The zebra is generally based on a setting of 80-95 IRE (Institute of Radio Engineers).

Think of 0 IRE as total black and 100 IRE as total white, indicating

The clouds in this shot are too hot to handle and display the "Zebra" pattern to warn of clipping.

the maximum amount of voltage that the system can handle. While film can quite often record these values, NTSC video considers black at 7.5 IRE units (usually called the pedestal in post-production and set-up in the field), and white at 80-95 IRE.

If you can set your zebra indicator to start clipping at 70-75 IRE you will be able to maintain detail in the brightest areas of your projected image. If you push it into the 90-95 IRE level, the brightest areas of your image will be little more than splotches of light with little or no image information in them.

At the lower end of the contrast problem are the blacks. Just as the high-intensity whites will have a tendency to blow out when projected or printed to film, so too will the blacks have a tendency to crush and go all black. The human eye is really the culprit here. We look at a scene and can make out the detail in the shadows just fine.

Several months later we're sitting in a dark screening room arguing with our account executive about the huge black swaths that hide the subtle actions and details that we worked so hard to create.

Just because you can see it with the human eye, don't believe it. Just because you can still make it out on the monitor, don't believe it.

If you've got something going on in the shadows that you want the audience to share, make sure that information makes it to the screen by giving it far more illumination than you'd normally think it needs.

By keeping a close eye on the contrast ratios that you're creating within your scenes, you should hopefully arrive at the film printer with a slightly flat-looking video master and just slightly punchier if your goal is digital projection. Of course you've tested all this before hand, right?

A waveform monitor should always be the final arbitrator of the lighting values in your video image. It determines what is broadcast quality, printable or projectable by measuring the actual voltages of the video image and is often the first indication that your image is destined to have problems within your chosen distribution mechanism.

Rack mounted or digital desktop, big production or small, on location or on the set there is nothing like a calibrated signal to assure you of the best possible image.The WFM measures the level of the video signal as voltage and is capable of representing the image visually in several forms. The most common use is to monitor the pedestal and peak white levels of the video image.

Many software applications and non-linear edit platforms also have built-in signal diagnostics. These slightly more sophisticated systems generally include a vectorscope (V-Scope) in addition to the obligitory waveform monitor (WFM), which is helpful in determining the color timing of your video signal.

INTERIORS

I personally like interiors, while perhaps the majority don't. I especially like sound stages where everything is designed for the process of getting the shot. Interiors allow you much greater control over continuity.

When you're done shooting for the day, simply shut off the lights and lock up. Next morning everything's in the same place, the lights are all the same value, the actor's marks are still where you left them.

Don't have enough budget for a sound stage? Rent an old warehouse for a month or two. It not only gives you a place to build your sets but you can rig huge, stationary soft boxes that can be used throughout your entire production.

Several years ago we shot *Barb Wire* in the old Hughes Helicopter factory out in Playa Del Rey. Funkiest old building you ever saw but it gave the cast and crew a home base to work out of as well as an inexpensive location for the movie's production.

The look of the movie took on much of the look of the building. Many of the props were merely re-purposed materials we found lying around. It's not just funky, small-budget projects that use old hangars and warehouses either. During the same time, Independence Day was in pre-production in the even funkier adjacent building.

One of the big secrets to lighting a scene is to have plenty of room to move the lights and camera around. The more control you have over the light, the more control you have over the audience's perception of the scene.

Bare bulbs focused directly at your actors create a harsh environment and amplify the agony or torment that they may be experiencing while a collection of soft, diffused light sources create an atmosphere of peace and tranquility. When you're setting your lights, don't forget to turn the house lights off!

WRANGLING THE BEAM

There are essentially two kinds of light. The *key* light is the main source used to light the subject, while the *fill* light generally comes from an angle close to the camera and is responsible for filling in and softening some of the shadows caused by the key light.

The intensity of the key in proportion to the *fill light* determines the mood of the scene. A *high key* lighting setup creates a bright scene with a lot of highlights while a *low key* scene has a much higher ratio of lighting and creates a much darker and visually more contrasting scene.

The basic rule of thumb states that the ratio of key light plus fill light should be 2:1 for prosumer video formats or as much as 3:1 in professional systems with higher resolving power.

It's a good idea not to exceed 4:1 unless you're going for a particular look, although some fantastic looks like those created in *Grind House* and *Sin City 1* and *2* have ratios that can reach 6:1.

Just about any introductory book on lighting will tout the *Three Point* lighting system. Don't. Problem is, light rarely if ever, falls in this configuration. While it remains a popular photographic (still image) metaphor where you're creating a representation, in motion imaging the light must echo the environment.

Lighting can also help create and define a style. Look at how the masterful use of high-key butterfly lighting helped sculpt the characters in Robert Rodriguez's *Sin City*.

The essence of good lighting is to initiate illumination from the general directions of the world you have created. Filter it, shape it, tint it, modify it, but the bottom line is that it needs to be MOTIVATED. It needs to have a reason for being there and it needs to come from the same general direction of that motivation.

One of the motion pictures that I shot since the last edition of this book is called *Closing Escrow*. It follows three quirky couples who collide when trying to purchase the same property.

As you might imagine with a small, independent movie about real estate, all of the locations were in actual houses. Since we were pretty much resolved to shooting without resorting to generators, the specific needs of limited power made for some very creative lighting scenarios.

Trish, Ron and An Tran lug some prototype lights from Arri into the location.

We shot *Closing Escrow* using two Sony F-900s, a couple Arri Light kits, a trunk full of *nickel and dimes* (assorted specialty lights), and a few prototype lighting instruments from Arri.

Our Key Gaffer, Trish Haremans, came up with some inventive ways to stretch the available power. Her observation: *"One of the niftiest additions to our lighting kit were several new instruments from Arri."*

My good friend and former Gaffer, Ron Sill (now with Arri in Hollywood), brought over some prototypes of their new line of tungsten-balanced Ceramic 250w lights.

Trish took an instant liking to the new instruments. As she put it: *"They not only came in very handy but they quite literally saved our asses because the 'X Light' open face unit (equipped with an intensifier and a grid cloth insert) gives off about 2K of light with only 250 watts of draw. Both the spread and fall-off were unusually even so we were able to light sizable areas using available house current.*

"Conventional lighting would have blown the entire neighborhood. Add to that the fact that even after several hours of burn, they're cool enough to break down after just a few minutes. Really amazing."

Not being one to let a good deed go unpunished we invited Ron to *"hang out"* for the day and light the kitchen. Since the location we were shooting that day was the newest and biggest house in the show, we had plenty of power to fire up a couple rooms at once.

Because of the many different reflective surfaces often found in kitchens, they are one of the hardest rooms in a house to light. Ron was up for the challenge and since we had seen him drive up in an Arri van, we figured that he might have a few extra instruments with him. After shooting out a scene in another end of the house, we headed over to the kitchen to see how Ron was doing.

We were all a bit shocked to see that he had incorporated a couple KinoFlo banks into his lighting build. I love Kinos as much as any DP but I mentioned that I thought it was a little strange that the #1 Arri lighting guy would build a system around a competitor's product.

"Since I was dealt this hand I played the cards. I looked at what was left in the lighting package and picked the stuff that would get the job done. On the set, it's not about brand names it's what creates the look, isn't it?" Touché, Ron.

The shot came out fantastic as you can see if you rent the DVD. Ron's lighting set-up allowed both the actors and the cameras a wide range of movement without annoying seculars and color shifts. Truly a master work of Gaff-ology.

On another feature production on which I served as director, we had numerous shots that involved various unique lighting signatures. My good friend Joe Di Gennaro served as DP and he devised an ingenious method of wrangling our light, which he explains:

"One of the easiest ways I know to maintain flexibility in lighting is to incorporate a dimmer system instead of relying on the traditional approach of using nets and scrims to control the light intensity.

"My standard choice is a pair of 100 amp 'twelve packs' containing 1.2K dimmers and another 100 amp 'six pack' of 2K dimmers.

Joe at the switcher. Play that funky music, White Boy.

"Although I have built my own system from the guts of an old AV studio, many film and theatrical lighting rental companies offer these items, which can be controlled by either a silicon rectifier panel, or with software driven by a laptop computer.

"SCR (silicon rectifier) dimmers only work with tungsten lighting, however. I was very pleased to discover that our Arriflex HMI lights had flicker-free, 'dimmable' ballasts, so he could control the intensity of the HMI lighting with the same flexibility as the tungsten; with the simple turn of a dial, instead of having to load the unit with scrims, etc."   ~ Joe Di Gennaro

When using a dimmer with tungsten light, the reduction in voltage causes a shift in the color temperature. We used this otherwise adverse effect to our advantage, incorporating the various colors of light in the design. Instead of adding an amber (CTO) gel to a light for a warm effect, Joe used a slightly oversized unit, and brought it down on the dimmer, which reduced the color temperature and generated a warmer light.

RAW SUN

The main advantage of sunlight over artificial light is that it is free, covers your entire scene and is quite easy to manipulate. The wide assortment of devices used for controlling and directing sunlight are generally far less expensive and easier to use than other forms of illumination.

These simple tools allow you to diffuse, cut, bounce and generally mold the light to do your bidding.

While direct sunlight can be harsh in a filmed environment, in a video environment it's downright catastrophic. The intensity of the sun's illumination isn't the only problem that it causes. It moves. Steadily and continuously the sun sweeps across the sky all day long. Shots you took in the morning sun won't always cut into shots at the same location later in the day.

If, like everyone else in the industry, you look at your dailies in the order shot, rather than sequentially, you probably won't see the problems until weeks or months later in editing.

When you spend several hours shooting someone's dialogue first thing in the morning and then come around to shoot the other persons dialogue after lunch, the sun and all of its bounces and secondary volumes will have moved.

That amount of time span creates an enormous gap of believability. The audience may not know what's wrong but they'll know something's not right. While they've stopped to figure out what the problem is, they aren't following your story.

The oldest and most wildly used accommodation for mellowing out direct sunlight is cloud cover. Often called *God's silk,* cloud cover generates a mellow, diffuse light that records well on film or video. With film, this is generally all you need but with video you should also introduce a bit of *fill* to keep your subject from going flat.

The least expensive way to bounce light is with the metallic coated cardboard called *showcard* and foam-core art-board which can be picked up at any art store. The more professional (and more costly) spring-loaded *hoops* generally have one side white and the other either shiny silver or gold.

Next up the food chain are the Matthews style metal frames that have been part and parcel of the filmmakers grip kid for nearly a hundred years. They are normally attached with common grip head to C-Stands.

SHAFTING

In sunny southern California, it is often easier to *shaft* sunlight into a location than it is to get the neighbors to sign off on generators. Since I very often shoot in the high income areas of Los Angeles, I've become quite proficient at shafting ... no laughing please.

In this image we are using a full range of bounces which include from far left; an 8' x 8' silk that is bringing the overhang up two stops, a soft gold reflector in a locking yoke that

The famous neighbors don't like production in their back yard.

is aimed at the actor, and a 12" x 12" mirror that is shafting a solid beam through a window and into a silver showcard that is lighting the background. At far right is a silver reflector on a locking yoke that is shafting through a piece of bubble wrap, into an 8' X 8' Lisa Marie (silver and gold checkerboard reflecting cloth).

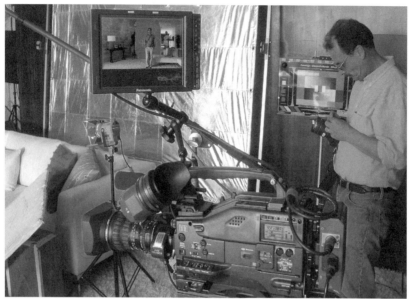

Veteran ILM Visual Effects Super Lanny Cermak checks measurements.

The image above shows the room that we were bouncing the light into from the previous picture. The shoot was for a Wii commercial that features a kid playing the *Pirates of the Caribbean: At World's End* game with characters from the movie.

Because of all the CG and compositing that needed to be done to the footage, ILM had requested that I use low key lighting to shoot the spot with.

Once hit by the bubble-wrap-diffused shaft of light, the Lisa Marie (which can be seen leaning against the far wall) provided an evenly textured volume that lit both the actor and the pop-up green screen which can hopefully be seen in the F-900Rs monitor.

If the printing gods are on our side, you might also be able to make out the volume from the 12" x 12" mirror shaft, lighting the deep background.   *(Note: the actual image was slightly brightened for printing.)*

Shafting is also invaluable in environments where electricity is dangerous or in short supply as well as places that are too cramped or oddly shaped to build a good volume in.

There is a place in the Hollywood Hills that legend says, was custom built for shafting. After shooting there nearly a dozen times, I'm beginning to agree. The caves were dug through the bedrock for the 1922 motion picture *Robin Hood* with Douglas Fairbanks.

They've since been used as the *'Bat Cave'* in the classic *Batman* TV series (hence the name), as well as in *Bonanza, Star Trek, Fantasy Island, The Lone Ranger, Gunsmoke, Wild Wild West* and countless movies.

There is a curve in the shaft so that you can't actually see through the mountain, but a side shaft allows you to hit any area in the cave with two or three shaft bounces.

Deep in the Bat Caves, camera operator Greg Solomon sets up at the cross-over of three shafts.

PERSONAL KIT

Even though the production company will most likely bring in a grip truck, it is always nice to have a small kit of your own.

A personal grip kit for an occasional shooter should include a gold and silver bounce, a diffusion panel of some sort and a few screens along with three or four C-stands. Don't forget to pick up a couple sandbags to keep everything upright.

When you don't have good cloud cover, or the clouds are small and sporadic, its time to pull out the diffusion panel. You can buy these large panels of translucent material ready made or make them yourself out of some PVC pipe and an old Army surplus parachute.

With a nice bounce fill on your actor's faces, and a silk diffusion above them to keep the direct sun at a minimum, you'll probably find that the background is a bit hot. This is where a nice big black net comes in handy.

Either single or doubled, the *net* has the ability to help manage the ratios between your subject and the environment.

The difference between a shot in direct sunlight and one done in diffuse light is quite dramatic as you've seen if you followed directions earlier on.

A double 8X8 net, a 4X8 topper and a 4X4 gold/silver bounce fill is an essential combo.

There are quite literally a hundred different ways you could put together a little personal kit. For those who don't live in a city with a good production gear store, I'd like to recommend *www.filmtools.com* in Burbank. They've been taking care of us Hollywood guys for quite some time.

I'm a big fan of the Westcott, ScrimJim system for a number of reasons. It is very compact, incredibly light, unusually sturdy and relatively inexpensive. It also doesn't make you look like a total geek when you pull it out on a location shoot.

The portability of the ScrimJim system in the above shot makes for a good choice since the entire kit is big enough for many shots, sets up and breaks down quite easily and can easily fit in the trunk of a car with enough room for a camera, tripod and assorted grip equipment.

COLOR TEMPERATURE

Color is expressed in terms of color temperature and essentially ranges for our purposes between the 1,500/K of a candle flame up to the 30,000/K of a crystal clear, high-altitude northern sky. The most relevant color temperatures that film and video makers deal with are:

60-watt household bulb @ 2,800/K

Film studio lights @ 3,200/K

Photoflood lights @ 3,400/K

Sunset in Los Angeles @ 3,000 to 4,500/K

Noon summer sunlight @ 5,400/K

HMI @ 5,600/K

Blue sky light @ 10,000/K

THE SPECTRUM OF LIGHT

The other problem with sunlight is that it changes color throughout the day. This is generally something that you can't see with the human eye unless its sunset or sunrise.

Imagine that you're shooting in a huge domed filter that is red at both horizons, bright yellow at the 45s and white *top dead center.* Generally these types of color density shifts are taken care of in the color timing stage of a film's production. With digital video this means that you've got to add another very time-consuming step to the processing of your images.

ARTIFICIAL LIGHT

Basically, light looks white to the human eye. That's because we have a mechanism in our brain that actually corrects for color shifts in the environment around us. It's actually rather unnerving when you realize how inaccurate the human eye is at determining color.

Ever notice someone's window from outside at night when they're watching TV? It has an intense blue glow to it while the window right next to it may have a reddish cast and the one next to that golden.

From the street our brain will actually see the broad variations in color generated by various lighting mechanisms because we don't have a specific color reference to lock on. If we were to walk into that house and into the room with the television in it, everything would appear quite normal.

Our brain knows the inherent color scheme of the environment and corrects accordingly. As we move from room to room, the same location that we saw generating a reddish hue will also seem normal as will the room with the golden cast.

With film we must constantly monitor the color temperature of lights. Many lights actually change color over time as the elements warm up. Corrective filters must then be added to get the various lights to match.

Many Americans who shoot in foreign countries are shocked by the lack of consistent electricity. The vast majority of the world uses far less electricity than we do. Even with converters and power conditioners, lights may run much less efficiently which causes red shift.

Open face lights deliver a much more efficient beam than lights with lenses. When selecting a lighting kit for questionable locations, you can't go far wrong favoring open face instruments.

There are two main film types which are balanced to the light source frequencies of tungsten (codeB at 3,200/K) and daylight (codeD at 5,600/K). Scenes lit with sunlight will appear normal when using a camera white balanced for daylight, while scenes lit with 3,200/K studio lights will appear normal when shot on a camera white balanced for tungsten.

If you were using studio lights to enhance an outdoor scene that was using the sun as the key light, you would need to put blue gels over the lights to balance their color temperature.

If you're shooting inside using studio lights as your key then you would need to put orange gels over the windows to balance the natural sunlight coming in the windows.

Many cinematographers in this situation will choose to shoot a daylight film and correct the key lights to daylight or use a timed lighting source such as the neon KinoFlo.

In many instances you will find that various lights have different color temperatures. It is a good idea to actually videotape all of the locations that you plan on using at night, prior to starting production.

Different lights will require gels to balance their color temperature. A fluorescent light next to an incandescent table light may create a noticeable and unwanted effect.

ArriLite 2000 Open Face   *Arri Junior 5000 Fresnel*

While there are tuned and tinted bulbs that can be placed in conventional sockets, the most common practice is to wrap fluorescent tubes with gels. Within a fixture it is also possible to have several neon tubes each generating a wide range of color temperatures from pink to bilious green. Needless to say, lighting is better done prior to the non-gaff crew and actors arrival.

THE QUALITY OF LIGHT

Light controls every aspect of what we do and the care that we take with it will either enhance or detract from the perceived value of our final product. We are storytellers and we tell our stories with light and sound.

Take away the light and all you've got is a radio show. We paint with light. It gives depth and presence to the scene and it creates mood. In order to paint with light you first need to see it in all of its nuance and spectrum.

The quality of light that is used in film production is developed and controlled by a small army of people who have spent the bulk of their lives refining methods and techniques for diffusing, redirecting and creating moods within the visual spectrum of illumination.

There are hundreds of lighting systems from the enormous *HMIs* to the tiny *Inky Dinks*, incandescent, luminescent and strobe; each offering its own particular palette of luminance.

Modern video technology creates a recording environment that can shoot in a wide range of brightness values but has far less sensitivity than film.

This doesn't mean that it records more colors or subtle shades than film but rather thatit is capable of recording in much a much wider range of light intensities.

Some video cameras are capable of shooting in situations where the human eye is even incapable of seeing. This gross latitude (that's 'gross' as in encompassing) that is inherent in the digital video environment is one of the primary reasons that video always looks so non-dimensional.

One of the most unfortunate hallmarks of a digitally acquired image is that it all too often looks quite flat. The need to dimensionalize your scene and pull the characters away from the background is perhaps the most essential of elements that go into your look.

Dimension is not a naturally occurring component of acquisition formats with limited latitude, so a substantial amount of craft must be used.

PAINTING WITH LIGHT

Spend a little time browsing the paintings of the masters. Their whole world was tied up in the quality of light. Look at the way they handle shadow and form. By using light to define regions within the compositional framing of the shot we can create an enhanced perception of depth and dimension.

Look at the shadows. Are they hard or soft, do they fall off rapidly or continue on? What angle are they coming from, what color is the light that caused them? The quality of light is often best described by the shadows it casts and the first step towards *seeing light* is in recognizing the importance of shadow.

As I've said before, lighting ratios are what define character in a monocular world.

Just getting the right balance of light to illuminate your scene is only the start. Light is the essence of the scene. It creates the mood and atmosphere of the

Ever since we found him in the ASC men's room with this thing, Dave Stump has been trying to convince us that it helps judge the quality of light.

environment as well as helps to develop the character of the actor. A well-lit scene is often a combination of direct, diffused and bounced light sources.

One of the goals of good lighting is to separate your actors from the background without resorting to making them brighter than the environment.

By using a slightly warmer color temperature (orange/CTO) in the background, your character will come off of the screen with more dynamics, and by using a cooler background temperature (blue/CTB) they will create a warmer, more intimate sensation with their performance. In addition to creating a context and mood, using different color temperatures gives your scene dimension and keeps your actors from becoming part of the scenery.

A small direct light source directly above the camera (eye light) gives life to the actor's eyes while a direct intermediate spot directed at the back of the actor's head (hair light) helps to separate them from the background.

A broad diffuse or bounced light source behind the camera can keep light from direct sources like the sun from creating deep shadows around the eyes and is, in itself, essentially non-directional.

One of the best exercises for lighting the human face is to put a couple of those realistic Halloween character masks on a couple wig dummies and then practice with various lighting set-ups.

For adding a really high-quality look to close-ups, try putting a strong, highly diffused light source above and slightly forward and to the side of the face. Take care to *cut* the light so that it doesn't hit the lens.

Since light falls off at a square of the distance, the soft contrast ratio that this setup creates is quite attractive, especially when shot with a medium long lens.

As foolish as this exercise may sound, by the time you've figured out how to get that rubber mask to look good you'll be ready for the big time.

PERSONAL STYLE

Lighting style is particular to the individual. Some cinematographers like to pull out every light they have access to and then fiddle with them for hours. I've worked with people like this and it is a costly and frustrating affair for everyone involved. I've also worked with DPs who can do amazing things with very few lights.

One strong beam can be redirected and shaped into incredible environments by people who can actually "see light." I won't explain this, but I guarantee that you'll fully understand when you get it.

Before learning to visualize light as volume, many people are amazed at how flat their images look when they finally see them projected. While our eyes view the set and actors in stereo, we are dealing with an essentially monocular system of recording and display.

A quick and easy solution is to look at a scene through only one eye before you shoot it. A viewing filter will enable you to see contrast ratios and lighting balances much more clearly.

LIGHTING THE SCENE

In order for a performer to appear sincere, he/she must feel comfortable within the confines of the set. In order to maintain that level of comfort, an actor should feel free to be a bit spontaneous and not be *"nailed down"* to a rehearsed choreography because of technical limitations.

For the caveman comedy *Homo Erectus*, we had to shoot for several days more than a quarter mile underground in the Longhorn Caverns in Texas. The long haul, the narrow passageways, poor ventilation and limited power made for a very challenging shoot.

The main living area for our quirky tribe of cave-people was in a large domed vault.

To bring the ambiance up to a base exposure level we floated a balloon with a 10K HMI up to the top of the huge chamber.

Luckily the interior of the cave was light-colored limestone which gave us a nice falloff and bounce that filled the vault with a warm, low key volume.

Since we were well below the surface ventilation was a real concern so much of the *"roaring campfire"* that the script called for was done using Arri 1K heads on flicker boxes, over which we later composited campfire elements that were shot at matching angles. We also placed small lighting units in the fire ring to motivate the light on the faces.

We used a number of under-lit silk blower pots (the kind you get from Spencer Gifts around Halloween) to simulate wall lights which added to the ambient volume and gave a very warm depth que to an environment that needed all the dimension we could give it.

Now that we had a workable volume of soft light filling the chamber, small pools of motivated torch light framing the walls and the motivated flicker of the central campfire, we could block the actors with conventional 1K instruments and scrim and filter conventionally.

Since the volume encompassed the entire vault, the actors were free to move as the muse hit them.

In one particular scene where David Carradine was pacing back and forth while pontificating, we simply *Hollywood-ed* (physically moved the gear by hand), his face light and the volume from the balloon filled the rest.

If we had used smaller lighting units, closer to the action, we would have had difficulty maintaining exposure, and would also have run the risk of crowding the actors' movements with equipment.

VOLUME DYNAMICS EXERCISE

As an exercise in the subtle dynamics involved in lighting, rig a light a few feet above you as you sit in front of a mirror. Rig some method of focusing the light (aluminum foil barn doors) straight down so that it creates a pool of light a few feet wide on the floor and then put a dark towel on the floor where the light hits so that there is little reflected light

Turn off all other lights and sit under the beam while looking at your reflection in the mirror. Notice the harsh manner in which your face is illuminated. Now, cup your hands as if you were scooping up a handful of water and slowly bring them up under your face.

For the smaller spaces in the caves we used a 5K balloon ...

Notice how the deep shadows under your nose and eyes are disappear-

... but for the main living area, the 10K balloon filled the space with a warm, highly textured volume.

ing and the almost luminescent quality that this organically diffuse, reflected source brings to your face.

Play with light. Experiment with it, bounce it, cut it, and figure out ways to diffuse it and make it do your bidding. Sit to the side of the beam and use white paper or cardboard to light your face using only reflected light. Notice how much softer and controllable the results are. As imperative as good lighting is to the conventional film production, it is even more important to video-to-film productions.

When you finally learn to *see light* you will truly become a cinematographer. Factors like resolution and platform will become less important to you than the quality of illumination.

People who don't share your passion will muse at your predisposition to tweak your shots and fiddle with the lights. To them it will seem excessive. In the end, long after the inconvenience of your efforts is forgotten, there will be a recording of dimension and persona that will underscore everything you've done.

CHAPTER 7

CAST 'N' CREW

As much as you might like to think of yourself as the lone desperado out there shooting away, it's almost impossible to create anything of lasting value in a vacuum. The people who buy into your graphic hallucination are trusting you to take care of them. It's not just a legal obligation, but a moral one as well.

There are a lot of shortcuts that can save you time and money. Low-budget moviemaking involves a seemingly endless re-negotiation of your bottom line. Accommodations are invariably made, things are done without, but I've yet to meet a successful filmmaker that didn't take the well-being of his cast and crew very seriously.

I'm not a big fan of clubs, especially when they're exclusionary. Even so, I recently shot my own movie under full industry/SAG contract, not because I'm a flag-waving union type guy, but because I respect my cast and crew.

Although I often get labeled as *"wildly independent"* I feel that it is important to point out that I'm a card-carrying member of the International Cinematographer's Guild (ICG), IA Local 600, Society of Motion Picture and Television Engineers (SMPTE), the Visual Effects Society (VES), and the Digital Cinema Society (DCS), and signatory to WGA, DGA and SAG. I don't do it to get work or be a member of a club, I do it for the protections and benefits that it offers my cast and crew.

Making a movie is a hard job, and dangerous too. By working under industry guidelines and regulations, my cast and crew were covered by workman's comp (insurance), and their retirement funds were paid into.

Now trust me on this, I didn't pay out any exorbitant salaries, and working with SAG is nearly as hard as making the movie — maybe harder — but the important thing is that my people were protected. Nothing else in the entire production process is that important.

More than anything else — more than resolution, more than budget, more than box office gross — it is your concern for your cast and crew that determines your professionalism.

So I guess that this is as good a time as ever to bring up the topic of the DGA. Yes, it's a dinosaur. Yes, it's exclusionary. Yes, it is expensive to join. I'm sure as an indie filmmaker, the DGA is about the last thing on your mind, but here's my thinking on this.

As a professional moviemaker you've got considerations that the hobbyist doesn't need to bother themselves with: PROTECTIONS, CONNECTIONS and CLOUT.

As a director on a low-budget film you are in a very vulnerable position. Something goes wrong, you could be paying for it for the rest of your life.

As a professional moviemaker, you're probably in need of some legal and financial protection as well. While organizations such as the IFP are a tremendous assist in getting your career off the ground, once you're off and running, the playing field changes rapidly.

Since you're probably not punching in nine to five at the office, you'll need a health plan, maybe even a nice little pension plan. No, you aren't immortal.

With the vast majority of low-budget, independent features, the director is seldom working for a salary. If the movie does well, he's promised a piece of the action. Cable television and DVD distribution have created a highly profitable distribution channel for independent work, but these are all large corporations that only see the bottom line. You need some way to track the money that is due you and then have enough clout to collect. To do that you'll need the playground bully on your side.

Contrary to popular belief, the Guild has long been a resource with open doors for the independent moviemaker. Now, with many of the old guard passing on into retirement, the Guild has been forced to reevaluate its position.

The DGA Independent Director's Committee has sculpted out a unique package of support for the independent that offers the same essential protections enjoyed by the big guys.

The golden days of the film industry are giving way to the pixelated vision of a digital future. Proximity to Hollywood is not a concern; on the contrary, production seems to be making a concerted effort to get as far away as possible. I just think that it's kind of cool, when the dinosaurs come down to graze with the rest of us cattle.

THE AUTEUR

The word *auteur* gets bantered around a lot these days: one person who can do it all. People try to hang that moniker on me from time to time and it always makes me cringe. I've been a cameraman my whole life and I've had the good fortune to shoot for some of the greatest directors in the business, but when it came time to make my own movie, I got my buddy Joe Di Gennaro to shoot it. Why? Because I have a number of very talented and well respected actors in my project. They were all familiar with my work and reputation in the industry. They trusted me to make them look good, not only physically as the camera sees them but professionally as the audience sees them.

There is no possible way that you can do justice to great actors by both shooting and directing them. Moviemaking is a collaborative process, and just because you can do every job in the entire manufacturing process doesn't mean that you should do them at the same time.

Of course there is Robert Rodriguez, who gets as close to being an auteur as anyone I know. His book *Rebel Without a Crew* is perhaps the perfect counterpoint to this one since we both possess similar skill sets, are both proficient cinematographers, can write our way out of a wet paper bag, and both know our way around a digital post-production environment.

Robert and I were standing at the Valet (this is Hollywood after all), following an interesting lunch where we were discussing the methodology of one of his upcoming productions. As we waited for our cars to arrive, he pulled out his wallet and showed me his rather impressive array of guild membership cards: WGA, DGA, the whole enchilada.

Robert takes great pride in the fact that he is a bona fide, soup-to-nuts filmmaker and in my experience, he is the only exception to the rule. Having seen him work, I can tell you that his secret is to surround himself with consummate professionals and then orchestrate his production like a battle plan out of Sun Tzu's *Art of War.*

But, hey: you don't have a cadre of highly gifted artisans to surround yourself with, and the last time you read the *Art of War* was, well, never. Your best chance of success is to weed out the most brutally honest and excruciatingly practical production methodology that you can find.

You'll need to look deep into the mirror of reality and scrutinize your natural proclivities. Be on the lookout for people who you feel possess your missing traits and then plead with them to buy into your little machination. These people are your partners, confidants, collaborators and could very well be your key to success.

Since they also possess skill sets that are markedly different from your own, they will also be an unending source of blinding insight as well as consummate frustration.

The idea is to never have more than one or two slashes (writer/producer/director) between your job descriptions at any one time. Those who bite off too big a chunk, always seem to choke on it.

It is good to have people who you admire, but there is a fine line between admiration and emulation. Just as the latest Nike sneakers won't really make you fly through the air like Michael Jordan, an HDV camera and the latest version of Apple's FinalCut won't turn you into Robert Rodriguez either.

There is a vast and fundamental difference between advertising mythos and reality. You step over that line without comparable talents and you're just another chalk outline on the boulevard of dreams.

NO MAN IS AN ISLAND

Moviemaking is a process that involves alternative points of view. In addition to sage organizational and financial counsel, a healthy dose of dissension is one of the more important ingredients that a good producer brings.

Controversy stimulates creativity and without it you become stagnant. No matter how blindingly brilliant you think your idea is, no matter how proficient you think you are at the craft of cinematic one way narrative, without an experienced "second opinion" your project stands a very good chance of becoming little more than self-indulgent drivel.

Not just the curse of emerging moviemakers, the discount bins are full of direct-to-video flops from people who simply should have known better. Arrogance, insolence, you can call it what you will, but the filmmaker who refuses to seek out alternative points of view is captain of a sinking ship.

Many of the grandest failures are simply credited to psychological or emotional problems when in fact the problem is more often than not physiological in origin. Many of the various jobs in the moviemaking process require a variety of both right and left hemisphere functions. It is very difficult to transition from the mindset of budgetary concerns to the mindset of writing a line of dialogue or setting a shot.

The most successful people always seem to surround themselves with those who possess an alternative point of view and the chutzpah to express it.

ALL YOU NEED IS GAFF

If we were to list the six most important jobs in the order of their importance to the fabrication of a successful motion picture, it would look like this:

#1 - PRODUCER

#2 - GAFFER

#3 - WRITER

#4 - DIRECTOR

#5 - SOUND RECORDIST

#6 - CAMERA OPERATOR

You might find this list a bit odd, especially coming from a person who is a working DP and whose job title isn't even on the list.

Despite their protestations, most producers would make fairly good directors, and nearly all gaffers are very capable camera operators. That's all you really need if you've got a good script.

If you're just starting out and really don't have the resource for a professional crew, please consider pulling in a working gaffer, if only as a consultant. Heck, make 'em a producer or DP or director. It is the one craft that will make the most difference on the screen.

To be a working gaffer you need to understand both the physical and emotional aspects of lighting as well or better than most DPs.

... most producers would make fairly good directors and nearly all gaffers are very capable camera operators ...

You need to understand blocking better than most directors and you need to have an almost photographic memory with respect to continuity. There simply is no more important job in the actual production process outside of gathering the money to make the movie.

A FORMULA FOR SUCCESS

Just because you've got a limited budget doesn't mean that you need to limit your resources. The knee-jerk reaction of most people starting out on their first cinematic venture is to put a crew together from friends and family. They're free, they put up with you and you'll be in a position to boss them around. What could be better.

There are so many physiological peccadilloes involved with this approach that it isn't even worthy of a gratuitous acknowledgment. By using friends you're merely repurposing whatever little social group manifestation pre-existed. Social groups are usually quite democratic; moviemaking is not.

By making a movie with your friends you'll constantly be striving to maintain the group dynamic — except, of course, this time you're the king. Well, it doesn't work that way for a number of reasons.

By upsetting a preexisting group dynamic you force an inherent restructuring that negates your chance of a stable production environment. Since you probably won't be using top-notch actors, you're going to need all the stability you can muster.

Perhaps most importantly, the chances are slim to nonexistent that your little group of friends contains all of the talents that are necessary to fully engage a successful manufacturing campaign.

By actively seeking out excellence in all aspects of the craft you must go outside your immediate group of friends. Again, a resource such as IFP is invaluable in assembling a team that actually has a chance at creating a successful product.

Try to limit the number of hats you wear and look for people who are passionate about developing their craft.

The writer that rejects the cliché and creates characters that constantly evolve and engage the audience's deepest, unresolved emotions will always find more than their fair share of success.

> Try to limit the number of hats you wear and look for people who are passionate about developing their craft.

The director that allows the actor be in the moment, thinking real thoughts and feeling real feelings right in front of us will connect the audience in a way that will seem like magic.

The cinematographer that uses his light to paint the spectrum of emotions across the pallette of the human face will bring life and vitality to his characters.

The producer who makes good choices, picks good people and then gets out of their way so that they can tell their story will be financially rewarded.

What are your goals and objectives? What inspires you? Scrutinize your motives. Do you have a passion for storytelling? Are you drawn to celebrity? Are you merely fascinated by the technology? Do you love working with other talented, passionate people towards a collective goal, or are you just looking for a good way to get laid?

Let's face it, directing is one of the only professions where you're treated like a god. People scurry about to do your bidding and the power you wield, if only in your limited kingdom, is as close as most mortals come to omnipotence.

Many successful actors are quite simply people in search of a personality. A vast majority of industry personnel embrace the production crew as a surrogate family while others seem to be here merely because they've proven themselves unqualified to do anything else.

As many people as there are in this glorious industry, there are an equal number of motivations. The secret is not in following your dreams but rather in following your proclivities.

Like a great painting by a true master, the cinema combines a duality that spans the spectrum of the human condition. From the greedy lawyers to the gregarious gaffers and grips, this industry embodies the most robust assortment of characters found anywhere. The secret lies in finding your natural place within the process.

GET A GRIP

First thing to do is ask yourself what you see yourself doing. What are your goals and objectives? Sure, it's your idea, and probably even your script, but are you really the best person to direct or shoot it?

Maybe since you have the *Big Picture* the project would be far more successful if you acted as Executive Producer or let someone else take a pass at that "gem" of a script.

It's great if you enjoy making movies, but if your project doesn't make money, or you don't pay back the people who invested in your project, your future as a moviemaker is going to be severely limited.

There are a dozen major job descriptions in the conventional motion picture manufacturing process and they are each responsible for dozens of departments operating under them. Each of these departments breaks down and branches out to tens if not hundreds more job titles given the size of the budget.

On projects with severely limited budgets many of these jobs can be combined, allowing a single person to wear multiple hats.

The problems start when, in the name of budgetary limitations, one of these jobs is eliminated rather than absorbed. The resulting hole in your organization can sink your project before it's even had a chance to leave the dock.

THE PROCESS

Starting from the point of view of a conventional, moderately budgeted, 35mm motion picture production and continuing on down to the ultra-low budget "Lone Wolf" video project, we'll take a look at what the various jobs do and why they're each so important.

There are numerous ways to break down the motion picture hierarchy — Studio Boss, Executive Producer, Director, Writer and so on — in a linear fashion. The problem is that the organization of a motion picture isn't linear and not all people are around for the entire duration.

A writer is actively involved in the start of a project, many times even before a director has been attached. The editor, who in many ways has the final word, may not even know of the project until principal photography has been finished.

More often than not, the writer hangs around on the periphery, sometimes contractually obligated to generate the occasional script fix, and editors generally cruise into the dailies just to get an idea of what's going on.

The production process can also be broken down into the distinct stages of DEVELOPMENT, PRE-PRODUCTION, PRODUCTION, POST-PRODUCTION and DISTRIBUTION. Various job functions crossover through all five stages while some deal with only one or two stages in the production process.

DEVELOPMENT — This is the period in which the initial concept, whether for a motion picture or television show, is conceptualized, written and pitched, though not necessarily in that order. You could find yourself pitching a hairball concept or a full-blown script. You could be pitching for the $500 you need to bail your cameraman out of jail or 20 million dollars to make your next science-fiction extravaganza.

Once you've convinced someone to back your cinematic venture you've got to let all the good people who just anted up have their way with you. Don't take it personally, it's just the way they do it in this industry.

PRE-PRODUCTION — You've got your money, the scabs are healing up nicely and you're slamming together cast and crew, trying desperately to find a production facility out of the country so you can get away from all these studio creeps.

This is when the project takes on its timbre as the cast and crew becomes the woof and warp of the story's tapestry. Mistakes and shortcuts here will, quite literally, haunt you till the day you die.

PRODUCTION — *"Lights, Camera, Action!"* Once you're rolling the sheer inertia of the process begins to sink in. The train has pulled out of the station and it's a whole lot longer than you imagined. Every decision that you've made up to this point is now following you down the track and will continue to do so until you utter the final "Cut, it's a wrap."

POST-PRODUCTION — A lot of production people look at this as their time to come up for a breath of fresh air. It is technically the end of the initial manufacturing process. If you're a director or other heavily vested individual, you're swimming for the surface like everyone else but just before you break through, the editor, who's got this really big lung full of fresh air, grabs you by the ankles and drags you back down.

If the production process could be described as running around a cactus patch in bare feet, trying to stomp out small fires, the post-production process could be described as an endless, featureless exercise in cave dwelling. This is when every mistake you've made, every bit of coverage you didn't get, every time you said "we'll fix it in post" comes back to haunt you.

And your loyal cast and crew? They've all gone on lovely vacations, hanging out on beaches, and sipping margaritas. And you? You're sucking down two-day-old coffee in a building that should have been condemned at the last turn of the century, trying to figure out a polite way to ask your editor to increase his personal hygiene regime to twice a week.

DISTRIBUTION — Damn, just when all the wounds had healed from the development process, here comes a whole new herd of bison intent on having their way with you. They're called distributors, syndicators and network executives and every one of them thinks you've got a purdy mouth.

If you're really lucky, and the distributors like your movie, these beasts will set your movie up for exhibition, and if you're really, really lucky the audiences won't hate it.

Then one day the check clears the bank, you're out on the promo circuit, and all you can think about is gettin' back in there and doin' it all over again.

I guess I should apologize for my cavalier and somewhat jaded view of the time-honored process. Those who have yet to make their first sojourn into the bowels of the Hollywood machine might find my observations rather crude. Hey, write your own book.

WHO DOES WHAT

In the most typical industry parlance there is a dividing line of job functions in the production process. It is called, quite simply, THE LINE. You're either above it or below it.

Think of all of the people above-the-line as the people who don't get their hands dirty, while the people below-the-line are the ones who actually make the movie. So, above the line you've got all the producers, the writers, the director and the actors, while below the line hover all of the production staff and assistants to everyone above the line.

The basic rule of thumb is that the Producer hires everyone above the line while the UPM (Unit Production Manager) hires every one below the line. Think of a Production Manager as the below-the-line producer, or in military terms, the staff sergeant.

Simply put, they run the show. The job is one of the hardest, most important and least appreciated because it is a full-time battle to maintain a creative atmosphere in an environment that all too easily gets bogged down in technical minutiae.

There is a growing trend to call production managers *"associate producers,"* which to me is somewhat akin to calling Leonardo da Vinci a paint slinger. But hey, I guess when you're standing at a bar, trying to impress the hot blond that just walked in, it sounds a lot cooler to say you're a Producer than a Unit Production Manager.

So basically the UPM takes the script and develops the first budget that anyone really pays any attention to. He also figures out how many days the project should take to shoot and between the two factors, Time and Money, calculates the Production Value. Basically the UPM negotiates a formula as old as production: Price, Quality or Speed, pick any two.

The Directors Guild of America takes a much more succinct view of the UPM's functions, essentially stating:

"The Unit Production Manager, under the supervision of the Employer, is required to coordinate, facilitate and oversee the preparation of the production unit or units assigned to him, all off-set logistics, day to day production decisions, locations, budget schedules and personnel."

Of all the people involved in each of the five distinct processes of production, the UPM is one of the most important job functions. In many instances, a good UPM is far more important than a competent director.

Second in importance to the UPM is the 1st Assistant Director who actually does all the paperwork that keeps the production humming.

There are two things a production runs on: vast amounts of paper-work and junk food. In my years of production experience, I can't remember a craft services table that didn't have a half-empty canister of Twizzlers sitting on it. But I digress.

So the First is basically responsible for breakdowns and preparing the stripboard, the shooting schedules, day-out-of-day schedules, cast availability, call sheets, weather reports and is occasionally required to direct background scenes and supervise and direct crowd control.

While the First is doing all this work, the Line Producer is busy deal-ing with emergencies and trying to keep the show running while also trying to take credit for everything the UPM does.

A good Director is essentially an "allower." He comes on the set every day and allows everyone to do his or her job. More often than not, he's had little, if anything, to do with the script and almost nothing to do with securing financing, other than lending the credibility or infamy of his name to the process. Hopefully the director is an inherently good storyteller and is capable of guiding the collective consciousness of the audience.

Directors are essentially the keepers of the metronome by which the process evolves. It is their responsibility to translate the script into visual terms. There is however the one unfailing truth that good scripts direct themselves. Hopefully the producers hired a good cast-ing director who picked good actors that personify the roles. Then all that is left is for the director to put them in the right places so they can do what they were hired to do.

Of utmost importance to the look and feel of the movie is the Director of Photography (DP). For many years it was the cinematographer who actually ran the production. Only when the ASC (American Society of Cinematographers) went up against the far superior cunning of the DGA (Directors Guild of America) did the director emerge as the on-set boss.

For the director it can be, and sometimes is, their first day on the job, while the cinematographer, more with film than video, needs to have a lifetime of experience behind them.

The Director of Photography relies on his staff of gaffers and electri-cians to move lights and direct and modify the beams they throw. The best boy assists the gaffer in setting up the lights while the electricians make all the necessary electrical connections and maintain the power supply.

One of the more notoriously gregarious members of the production crew is the grip. Basically, anything, other than lights, that needs to be moved, one of these guys "grip" it and move it.

They are the handyman of the set, building scaffolding, placing props and creating unique devices to assist in various shots. If the camera is set on a dolly then it is the dolly grip that physically moves it.

In film productions and higher end video productions, the audio is recorded separately from the image. The sound recordist (sound man even if they're female) and his or her boom operator are responsible for recording not only the spoken sounds of the actors, but also a catalogue of ambient "room" sounds that will be used later by the editorial staff.

The script supervisor is essentially the director's brain. Rarely, if ever, are the scenes in a movie shot in sequential order. It is the script supervisor who is responsible for making sure that everything from clothes and hairdos to the position of the dead body matches the shot they did at another time. They are also responsible for making sure that the scenes have been shot from all the necessary angles that the script calls for.

Second Unit does stunts, effects shots, crowd scenes, battle scenes and generally shoots all the plates for later effects shots if there isn't a dedicated effects unit on the show.

At the very bottom of the heap are the lowest paid employees, the PAs (production assistants), otherwise known as gophers (go for this, go for that). Their job is to direct traffic, control access to the set, and go for stuff.

So that's a rather basic, albeit tongue-in-cheek, overview of the essential structure of your basic motion picture. Figure an average ten-million-dollar project will have a couple hundred people running around between several stages and locations. But hey, you don't have ten million dollars. That's why you're reading this book.

So now we gotta figure out how you can cram all those job descriptions into three or four people. First thing you've got to do is figure out who the most important people are. Simple: director, unit production manager, cinematographer, grip — and here's how we're going to combine the jobs.

DEVELOPMENT — Like the slimy caterpillar that is destined to evolve into a beautiful butterfly, the UPM starts out as an Executive Producer. He is like an organ grinder who, along with his trained monkey (cinematographer/director) raises the money and develops the script. The Executive Producer/UPM or the cinematographer/director in many instances is also the writer.

PRE-PRODUCTION — Congratulations, you've got your money, so now the Executive Producer starts to metamorphose into the UPM, looking for cheap, or better yet, free locations and an individual to actually take responsibility for doing the physical work (a.k.a. grip/ gaffer/PA). Meanwhile the cinematographer/director gets involved in casting.

PRODUCTION — Once you're rolling, the Executive Producer/ UPM assumes the script supervisor's position while the cinematographer/director arranges actors and along with the grip/gaffer/PA/soundman sets the lights and then finally shoots the scenes. Someone's wife or girl friend usually gets to be make-up/wardrobe/craft services; don't forget the Twizzlers.

POST-PRODUCTION — The cinematographer/director now becomes the editor because they're the only one who has been able to follow the erratic sequences thus far. The executive producer/ UPM/script supervisor becomes the script supervisor/assistant editor and helps keep track of where the various shots and elements are. The grip/gaffer/PA becomes a PA/producer/webmaster and develops potential distribution channels while fending off actors and vendors looking for their money.

DISTRIBUTION — Hopefully the PA/producer/webmaster has generated some significant interest and lined up some really good festivals as the three of you head off into the sunset with your hard-earned show and a half-empty canister of Twizzlers.

The cast and crew is the true equity of a production. They are the woof and warp of the tapestry you've spun. The degree to which you coordinate their efforts and protect their interests is the cornerstone of your professionalism.

The first time I met Pierre de Lespinois he was testing gear. Since then he has built one of the most advanced digital post production facilities in the world and created dozens of ground-breaking shows. His highly acclaimed series' for Discovery, *"When Dinosaurs Roamed America,"* *"Before We Ruled the Earth,"* and *"Dinosaur World"* marked significant leaps forward in both technology and methodology.

Pierre tests the signal quality of a new batch of gear.

Pierre has earned 12 Emmy nominations and won four including the first Digital Golden Laurel Award presented by the Producers Guild for the HD production, *"The Secret Adventures of Jules Verne."*

There are few people who have spent more time on the leading edge of digital production and done as well. During a recent test we were doing to compare some of the newer HDV gear to more conventional HD-SDI tools, he mentioned something that I feel needs repeating.

"In conventional analogue methodology, preproduction, production and post production occur in a linear form over three separate periods of time. Especially with production and post production, you pretty much shot everything on location and then you came back and built elements and started editing your film.

"We've found that by combining production and post production that we're not only getting a more efficient film but a much better film. The number of re-shoots goes way down and since we are there telling the story, the coverage and cut-aways and reversals all become a more integral part of the process.

"A digital set is a smarter place than an analogue set. More people have more information about what is going on. They have more instantaneous feedback about how their part of the process is fitting into the whole. Make up's a little too contrasty, or costume isn't taking the light correctly, you can see it there in the on set monitor.

"The nice thing about having monitors on set is that you're sharing the exposure, framing and movement information with the people who are helping you make your movie.

The old school, the film style approach was 'don't worry, I got the shot.' It was all about magical chemicals and job security. For me, the more eyes I have on a shot the better. I trust my crew, that's why they are there."

~ Pierre de Lespinois

CHAPTER 8

DIGITAL CRAFTSMANSHIP

Digital moviemaking parallels traditional filmmaking with the addition of understanding where and when accommodations for resolution, crew and production inertia must be taken into consideration. You've also got to have a firm grasp of both video and computer technology.

Combine this with a drastic reduction in the number of people among whom this expertise must be spread out and you'll realize that good digital film is potentially far more difficult to create. Not only do you have fewer people as a resource, but they each need to have a working knowledge of several aspects of conventional production methodology and then be able to incorporate the vague nuances of technology and budgetary limitations into the process.

Each aspect of the production process involves many years of evolution and refinement. It would be foolish to embark on a film project without having even a smattering of understanding with regard to the established methodology of conventional cinematic production. You won't just be wasting your own time but the time and resources of all those around you.

Even if you know in your heart that you are the rightful heir to the Spielberg throne, be humble.

Low-budget film production generates a lot of stress and frustration. Never enough money, never enough time, never enough of anything but problems. It's all too easy to let it get to you, and for you to start becoming a tyrant. As soon as this happens, you'll start losing momentum and all your mealy-mouthed apologies the next day won't get you back on track.

Always treat your cast and crew with respect. Take time to acknowledge their contributions and include them in decisions. Even if you know in your heart that you are the rightful heir to the Spielberg throne, be humble.

LINGO

Like all professions, filmmaking has its own languages. These languages or lingos are essential building blocks that are all too often overlooked or misused. The contemporary film production unit is a complex organization of numerous specialized groups interacting with a common goal.

The director needs not only to understand what each group is capable of doing but also how to communicate with that group so that his requests are understood. Of the many subset lingos involved in contemporary production, the four languages that the director must be fluent in are the Literary Language, the Actor's Language, the Production Language and the Visual Language. There are others, but these are the ones that I feel are most relevant.

LITERARY LANGUAGE

The Literary Language deals with character development, structure and timing. It is the vernacular of the screenplay. The essential foundation of any motion picture is described in this language in terms of empathy and structure.

Empathy is the essence of a good screenplay. Will the audience bond with, and care about, this character? All too often, the inexperienced writer reverts to a series of hysterics or gratuitous confrontations to get the audience worked up, but this is just a cheap imitation for the true craft of evoking the most powerful of audience connections.

A truly empathetic character portrayal will cause the viewer to project their own personality into the character's situation and live the story vicariously through them.

There really are no formulas per se, but rather a few battle-weary rules of thumb. Structure is the style of architecture by which your script is constructed. The essence of any script's structure comes down to its central theme.

In the simplest of terms, it is what the movie is about. Every element and character that you can attach to it moves your story along. The plot is the sequence of events that moves the characters along and creates the ups and downs that identify a good story.

The way you put it all together and the voice you use to tell your tale are the style. Great writers, great directors, great actors all have a style that sets them apart from the others in their field.

Audiences go to movies to experience situations and sensations that will generate strong emotional reactions and insights. The structure, the characters and the conflict of the script must engage the audience and give them a revealing insight into the human spirit.

A great script moves the audience along with a series of compelling visual elements (a picture is worth a thousand words) and uses the dialogue to glue the pictures together. This is true even if your movie never makes it any further than the internet. You must engage the audience!

All the technology in the world won't make up for a lack in the basics of cinematic storytelling. As filmmakers we've really only got two tools at our disposal: sight and sound.

Great writers, great directors, great actors all have a style that sets them apart from the others in their field.

Since digital moviemaking involves substantial sacrifices, particularly in the visual dynamics of the finished product, we must seize every opportunity in the production process to enhance the perceived value of our final product.

The essential unit of measure is the "shot," where an action or performance is recorded until the director calls "cut." A group of related shots create a scene, and a group of scenes form an act, of which there are generally three in a conventional motion picture. The shot is visually described by the angle from which it is recorded, such as subjective, objective or point-of-view.

Continuity is the flow of elements that carries the audience along. Good continuity never lets up or offers the viewer a chance to disconnect with the story.

Each new scene or location is established with a master shot that tells the audience where they are and hopefully how they feel about it. After the situation is established the camera moves in for a series of closer observations of the action or situations involved.

If the scene involves dialogue between two people, you might go in for a two-shot, which is a medium framing that shows the proximity of the two characters. You might then move in for a "close-up" of one of the characters faces or an "over-the-shoulder" shot to further explain context and proximity.

Continuity also deals with the essential time base of the film, the color palettes, physical direction, lighting and tempo of the action and eventually editing.

The lingo of editing is evolving daily as new production metaphors become accessible. Many of the terms from the mechanical age of film editing have made the transition into the digital age. Once a linen bag hung from a metal frame, the non-linear environment still uses the term "bin" as a holding place for shots and sequences.

The selection, arrangement and timing of the various shots into a continuous story is the essential goal of editing and the lingo that is involved spans the spectrum of narrative influence, timing and aesthetics.

ACTING LINGO

The Actor's Language is as varied as the methods by which they've learned their craft and many times you'll have actors from different schools on the same project. Developing a rapport and artistic bond with the individual actor is dependent on understanding what motivates them.

To even brush lightly upon this topic is to incur the wrath of acolytes of the various schools of acting, and the industry in general, but here goes.

In 1898, Constantin Stanislavsky founded the Moscow Art Theater, which was Russia's first ensemble theater.

"The program protests against the old manner of acting and against theatricality, against artificial pathos and declamation, and against affectation on the stage, and inferior conventional productions and decoration, against the star system which had been a bad affect on the cast, against the whole arrangement of plays and against the poor repertoire of the theaters." — Stanislavsky

Greatly inspired and influenced by Stanislavsky, Lee Strasberg recruited 30 actors in the summer of 1931 to form a permanent ensemble dedicated to creating social change through acting.

The newly formed Group Theater combined Gestalt psychology with the ensemble approach, which developed into a series of physical and psychological exercises called "The Method."

The purpose of these exercises was to break down the actor's barrier between life on and off the stage. If a part called for a specific emotion, the actor needed to recall the feelings and circumstance of a similar event in their life and then bring this honest emotion to the stage.Despite its relatively short life span, the Group Theater is perhaps the single most significant experiment in the history of American theater.

Along with Lee Strasberg, the group's founding members included Stella Adler and Sanford Meisner, who went on to found their own schools of acting.

The essence of these teachings is to give the actors tools by which they can access their own emotions in the unconscious mind.

Since the unconscious mind can't be controlled directly, students are involved in various exercises that are designed to evoke specific emotional correlates.

Even though the schools are all in some way based on interpretations of the teachings of Stanislavsky, their ideas are often considered to be in conflict with each other. Stella Adler's interpretation is considered closest to the original Stanislavsky, then Sanford Meisner, and then Lee Strasberg.

If I, a non-actor, were to attempt to describe the basic theme of the various contemporary schools it would be this:

Adler is built upon Imagination.

Meisner is built upon Immediate Experience.

Strasberg is built upon Sense Memory.

The British approach is built upon Observation.

The Meisner system seems to produce actors who pay attention to their partner better. Some of the basic Meisner exercises include the yes/no and various repetition and back-and-forth exercises that tend to *"bond"* the actors together. *"Acting is living life truthfully under imaginary circumstances." "The emotional life of a scene is a river and the words are the boats."*

The Strasberg, or Method, system tends to produce actors that are a bit more tightly wound. The system is based on Sense Memory, which is the process of recalling all of the attributes of an object, and Emotional Memory, which is the process of recalling significant events and situations from the actor's own past.

This produces the best actors for bluescreen and effects performances, but often at the expense of the actor's mental health. Stella Adler once said about Lee, *"He would push people into spaces that they should not go without a licensed therapist present."* Strasberg would often tell actors that they should get some therapy.

Personally I feel the best improv exercises use sense memory. It catapults you into a sense of belief. Privacy in public. *"Visualize a real situation in your own life and do your lines within that frame of mind."*

Stella Adler gives us the process of action verbs and is based on imagination as being the best motivation for a good performance. The imagination is very powerful in the presence of a director who loves to tell stories. *"Get the verb of it, don't worry about the emotional thread."*

The late Marlon Brando was an acolyte of Stella Adler and once told me that I should just do a chapter on her and leave it at that.

The British approach to acting is an odd one. Not that it doesn't generate spectacular performances or consummate actors, but rather it is based on the actual achievement of acting. Rather than becoming the character emotionally or mentally, the British system actually emulates a character by adopting all of the physical traits and characteristics.

ACTORS AND THEIR NEEDS

Music videos, although not necessarily an appropriate metaphor for cinematic construction, deal with limited bandpass constantly. Many people whose videos play regularly on MTV and VHI also have robust cinematic careers. Madonna, Will Smith, Sting and others are constantly dealing with the duality between film and video.

The almost unlimited latitude of film can generate thousands of gradations that constitute the range of expression, while most video only has several hundred shades of gray to work with. It is these subtle gestures and expressions that convey the hidden agendas and emotions that are so important to creating empathy and emotional connections.

Do your actors have more film or video experience?

One of the easiest and most effective ways to allow an actor to adapt his style to your environment is to tape improvisations. The important point to remember is to professionally light the set or area where the improv is to take place. The simplest method would be to stretch a large diffusion panel above the area with a few crossed key lights.

You're killing several birds with one stone here. You're getting the actors comfortable with each other and you're allowing them to metamorphose within the context of the production environment.

Generally in very low-budget movies someone's girlfriend or wife is the designated make-up person. This generally entails little more than a smack with the powder puff and some light colored lipstick for the guys while the gals always seem to want to do their own.

By videotaping the improvs and rehearsals you not only give the actors a chance to make modifications and adjustments, you also get an excellent opportunity to actually print a test if you intend to finish on film. Take your best shot directly to your film printer of choice and have them make a minute or two-minute projection test.

Don't worry about sound and 3:2 pull downs, just have them print a frame of video to a frame of film. Not only will you see just how much potential resolution and color space your chosen video format has to offer but you'll also be able to let your actors know how their make-up choices are transposing.

The goal of improv is to connect the subconsciousness of the character to the subconsciousness of the actor.

Imagine if you got all the way through production and post-production and finally up-converted and printed to film only to find that all of your actors looked garish. Oh, they looked great on the video monitor but up there on the screen…. Don't be foolish. The two golden rules of digital video:

Don't stop shooting. Don't stop testing.

There is a big difference between improvisation and rehearsal. Improv is an exercise in developing rapport between the actors and most importantly it creates a shorthand between the actor and the director. Once you start shooting you'll have so many things to keep track of that communicating with the actor will become a whole lot easier if you both have some previous common reference.

The goal of improv is to connect the subconsciousness of the character to the subconsciousness of the actor. A good improv should stress that there is no right or wrong approach. You simply can't do an improv incorrectly. Some may be better than others, but if you send your actors into an improv without obligations or judgments you'll end up with a much happier kennel of puppies.

Rehearsal on the other hand deals with the actor's attempts to identify the emotional truth and core of the character. This process is best not practiced too much because it can have the unfortunate effect of flattening out the performance.

Your actor may feel that they've got the character nailed and merely regurgitate it back for you, rather than struggle with it and let it evolve before the lens.

In the end, you're going to want to look for performances that are truly different and compelling.

PRODUCTION LANGUAGE

The Production Language essentially deals with the real-time business of making the connections, telling the story and getting the bills paid. This language starts with the budget and includes all the vagaries of finance and deal making on an extremely sophisticated level.

When you're dealing with studio or distribution company executives, they most likely will be throwing around business school lingo. Don't fake it!

What might sound like a really good deal in Harvard-ese might actually be the worst deal of your life. While there's no way to cram a six-year education into the development cycle of your movie, a great shortcut is to read the Friday copies of the Wall Street Journal and the Hollywood Reporter, front to back every week for a month.

The ability to make movies based on an innovative script is one of the primary motivations to the digital moviemaker, but if you're submitting your script to a studio, it often causes problems. As I've already mentioned, the studios don't actually make movies any more, they make deals.

As a result, the executives that your script must pass through are all lawyers or MBAs. A deeply revealing or emotionally insightful script is frightening to them. They're just not mentally equipped to deal with the subjective realities of deeply revealing interpersonal revelations.

Many of them try to adapt by finding ways to express subjective concepts quantifiably. There's always some new and tragically hip formula floating around Hollywood. It's like they all go to the same parties and hear the same neo-theological postulate and next thing you know you're sitting in a pitch meeting listening to the Harvard Business School interpretation of the mise-en-scene.

Instead of actually going out and developing promising actors, they merely recycle the "safe bets" to the point where you'll see the same faces in four or five movies a year. Is it any wonder that the growing trend is to write bigger and bigger effects into the script or more spectacular obstacles to the character's goals?

This formulaic, knee-jerk manner of writing is merely an accommodation to the sad lack of industry acumen.An independent script has far more latitude and should be wholly different than a studio script. There is no excuse for not developing the strong combination of revelation and sensation that creates the dramatic center of your script. The problem comes with the lack of subtlety that is available with digital productions because video simply doesn't have the dynamic range of film.

While motion picture film can capture the hundreds of thousands of subtle shifts in expression that echo pages of dialogue, the script destined to be shot in video must convey these thoughts more through speech and gesture.

The greatest challenge for the digital scriptwriter is to create a boldness of action that treads the delicate balance between too much and not enough.

Unfortunately, the dramatic center is based on subtle revelations and digital video is far from being a subtle medium. Instead of focusing on making the script or scene "commercial," concentrate on evoking a series of emotional responses from the viewer. Creating an atmosphere in which the viewer can emotionally bond with the character is perhaps the hardest and most important objective in a video-for-film or video-for-net script.

Don't keep the audience guessing about the character's persona. The more time it takes you to bond your audience to your main character's life and predicament, the more time they'll have to find fault with your film's technical shortcomings.

A 35mm feature can afford to spend time showing the audience around, getting them used to the environment and basically feeding them eye candy. You can't. Get down to business, get them involved and do it quickly. If you haven't sucked the audience into your world in the first few minutes, chances are very good, unless you've got a real barn-burner of a script, that you won't be able to reel 'em in at all.

It's not a bad idea to hold off on the title sequence until after they've had a chance to become vested in your principal characters. An even better solution is to suck in the ego a bit and put them all at the end. Titles are generally slow and plodding, a perfect time to analyze the quality of your image.

And once you're moving, don't let up: momentum is critical to the digital script. A 35mm film project can afford to back off of the action here and there and allow the characters to breathe and have those small moments that offer up deeper insight into their hidden motivations. Not you. Stay on 'em and don't let up. If you keep the audience involved in the emotional roller coaster of the story, they won't have time for anything else.

And when you're writing that witty repartee, don't forget to maintain a uniqueness in the character's voice. By keeping the lead's voice separate, you can keep it tied into the movie's dramatic center with less reliance on the audience picking up on the more subtle indicators that would generally be used in a film script.

Too often scripts become expositional in the third act, trying to tie up loose ends. This is the failure of establishing a solid base. Any basket weaver will tell you that a small mistake in the base will only get more noticeable as the basket progresses.

With digital moviemaking this is particularly dangerous because it lets your audience off of the bus before the movie is over. Any glitches or shortcomings that they missed earlier will leave with them.

Writing is a tough way to make a living. When its good, there are wheelbarrows of money coming through the door, but that's the exception. The reality is that it very often takes ten or twenty scripts to get one that is good enough to get turned down by a studio.

I have a half dozen friends who regularly get millions of dollars for their scripts, but the whole process always seems to exact a terrible tole. My good friend Erika Lopez puts it nicely when she cautions: *"Don't pick a writing career just because it fits nicely on a kitchen counter. An orange-juice can full of scalding-hot bacon drippings would be more fulfilling."*

DIGITAL DIRECTING

The process of storytelling is perhaps the oldest profession, yet the inherent dynamics that constitute a great storyteller are all too often misunderstood.

Moviemakers are predisposed to the one-way narrative and as such need to maintain a strong visual presence in our mind's eye of the texture and pacing of the story elements.

The director must also keep in mind the progression of various character arcs and how they interrelate, even though subsequent scenes in a picture might be shot months apart. This supernatural persistence of vision must often be maintained for a year or more and is all too easily ravaged by drug or alcohol abuse.

In order to tell a rich and compelling story, directors need to have experienced life from both the valleys and the mountaintops. This comes with maturity.

Look around at all of the truly great directors. They represent the full spectrum of the human condition yet they generally have one thing in common: maturity. You on the other hand are a brash young Turk with fire in your loins.

Take a lot of deep breaths. The pressure and anxiety the directorial process creates can kill a career before it's had a chance to screw up on its own. Much of the pressure of directing comes from trying to fix compounded errors.

You make a little mistake in casting or skimp on a location and then whenever it comes up, instead of addressing it you aggravate the situation further by trying to "work around" it. This compounding phenomena has taken down directors and their productions, large and small. Always, nip mistakes in the bud.

After years on the set I've come to realize that the vast majority of people who call themselves directors are merely playing director. They have opinions but no real unifying vision of original thought. They are driven by the urge to control more than the drive for creative expression.

It seems as though anyone who really wants to, can be a director once. The "one timers" are easy to spot; they have no understanding of blocking or the power of camera moves. They never have time to work on their craft, and they almost always make sure that their name is embroidered on the back of their "official" director's chair.

As annoying as a bad director is, they really don't impact the end product all that much unless they actually try to direct. As a control freak, they've probably developed a healthy set of managerial skills and they've hopefully got a good idea of where to put the actors.

Many great directors do little more than this and having cast good actors, need to do little more. The real harm comes when a "pretend" director tries to direct.

I've taken a lot of workshops and gone to a lot of seminars with respect to directing, and many of them were quite good. The most useful, however, was Judith Weston's *Director's Workshop* which is based on her highly recommended book Acting for Directors.

Among the many inspirational and unusually relevant exercises that our class performed was an exercise that identified the trademarks of bad directors. Occasionally I catch myself falling into those patterns when talking to an actor. For me, being able to identify detrimental methods of communicating with actors has been a powerful, although inexact, tool.

Now, for the first time I actually had a quantifiable metaphor with which to measure my interaction with actors. With Judith's permission I've condensed it down, paraphrased it, and am sharing it with you.

TRADEMARKS OF BAD DIRECTORS

• Result Freaks

"Can you make it funnier? Can you take it down a notch?"

This causes the actor/director relationship to turn into a guessing game and forces the actor into their "bag of tricks."

• Delivery Doctors

"Don't say, I love you, say I love you."

The director should be communicating the meaning of the line, not the inflection.

• Attitude Police

"Show me how much you hate this guy."

Forcing actors into an attitude corner is the difference between doing something and showing something. Forced attitude creates posturing which prevents the actors from listening to each other. Nothing devalues a performance more than actors that aren't paying attention to each other.

• Emotional Mappers

"OK, when you come through the door you're thinking that no one's home and then you hear something. You're disappointed because you wanted to be alone but you're scared because you think it may be a burglar."

Psychologizing or mapping the emotional terrain of a character is the ultimate control device, generally used by egotistic directors that don't trust their actors. Aside from being long-winded and tedious, this form of direction is counter-productive in an environment where time is at a premium. The result of this literal interpretation of the script will be a performance with no through-line.

• Process Servers

"I think your character is very happy."

As soon as an actor tries to have a feeling on demand, they look like an actor.

- ## Schizo

"He is happy but his heart is broken that she is leaving."

This pseudo-intellectualized method is intended to illustrate the complexity of the character. People are complex, they may say one thing while doing another, but they are not actually able to do two things at once. Divergent emotions cancel each other out and the actor ends up faking both of them.

- ## Judgmental

"He's an introverted geek" or *"She's a slut."*

Perhaps the most destructive device used for determining a character's make-up. Judgment forces the actor to telegraph the character to the audience "I'm the good guy" or "I'm the villain."

A director that uses this technique eliminates suspense by showing us the end of the movie when the character is introduced. In the end, the audience should be the ones to make the judgments.

Good direction generates behavior in the actor. It is sensory rather than intellectual and objective and specific rather than subjective and general. It describes experience rather than drawing conclusions about experience.

The best directors actually do very little directing, but rather guide with questions. *"What is important about this scene?"* *"What if the character just lost a family member?"* *"Do you feel like hitting him when he says that?"*

Howard Hawks used to say that he was merely giving the actors an attitude. *"Once they've got an attitude, then it's up to them to do the lines."*

There are, of course, as many styles of directing as there are directors. One of my favorite analogies with regards to the director's role is from Robert Altman. I apologize in advance for any misquoting as I was at a party when I heard him telling it and I wasn't in any shape to take notes.

Essentially he related making a movie to building a huge sandcastle. *"In the beginning you're all excited about the concept of building a sand castle, so you sit around with some other people and design the thing and plan where and how to build it.*

"Every one has a lot more opinions than you were expecting and the whole thing starts changing so much that by the end of the process you're almost ready to ditch the whole idea.

"Finally, the day comes that everyone planned on and it turns out to be a really nice day, so you go to the beach and start building the thing. With all those people trying to help it takes a lot longer to build than you thought it would.

"It's getting hot, you got sand in your shorts, it's looking totally different than what you had originally envisioned and you can't wait for the whole thing to be over.

"Finally, just before sunset, you finish it. People like it or they don't. A large wave comes along and washes it away and you're ready to start planning the next one."

FIRST-TIME DIRECTORS

The odds of actually creating anything of value on your first effort are so overwhelming that it should probably be up there with winning the lottery.

Here is a quick story about someone who beat the odds.

A few years ago Armen Kaprelian showed up on my patio with script in hand. He had a good pitch; not too long, it didn't wander and it had a point.

He had been producing a very successful show on the *Home and Garden Network* called *House Hunters* and had written a script that was not only fresh and clever, but it was about a topic he knew.

The script was called *Closing Escrow,* and it followed three couples on their quest to find the perfect home. Since the script was a comedy and he wanted to run as much improve as he could handle, he cast from *The Groundlings* improv company and local comedy clubs.

Armen put a very strong pitch package together and raised his

Armen runs the rabbit through its lines.

financing one handshake at a time. It was very impressive to watch him build on his plan and maintain momentum against some very impressive odds. More visionary than dreamer, Armen's no-nonsense approach solid background and strong moral compass made a very compelling package.

My good friends Randall Dark and Kristen Cox signed on as producers and a few months later we began shooting the move using two Sony F-900 cameras and a light grip and electric package.

Having the cable background, Armen wasn't flustered by budget limitations and constant location moves. On the contrary, he seemed to enjoy the challenge.

The principal production ended several weeks later and Armen began a year of cave dwelling. I poked my head in a few times here and there and each time witnessed a cut that was vastly improved from the former.

A year later, almost to the day, Armen calls with the news that *Closing Escrow* is a premiere selection in the *HBO Comedy Festival* in Aspen. It packed the house on its first showing and was called back for an encore the following day, which packed the largest theatre in Aspen again. *Closing Escrow* was promptly purchased for an undisclosed amount.

A month later the phone rings, it's Armen; he wants to drop off his next script.

So here we are on my patio again. Armen has just signed with a high-powered, Hollywood agency and I couldn't resist asking him for a few words for the book.

"I think the most important skill you should have as a director/filmmaker is the ability to listen. The image of a director is someone that's always yelling and telling people what to do. While you do need to be the one to assume the authority on the set, your priority is to make this the best possible scene for the film.

"There may be a better way to execute a scene than the way you initially imagined it. Maybe there's a better line she could say here, or maybe my DP has a good suggestion for this shot. You'd be a fool not to consider these options.

"More often than not, you'll reject the idea because it may not fit within the story's framework, and of course, sometimes you reject them because they suck. There were a lot of suggestions that I rejected during production, but at the same time there were great contributions from our awesome cast and crew. And the movie is better for it. It helps everyone to feel good on the set and vested in the project.

"The ability to listen is extremely important as long as you can discern the good ideas from the bad ones. That's why it is so important to surround yourself with talented people.

"This same mentality should be applied in getting the film off the ground. You want to listen to your attorney and your accountant to make sure you're setting up your business and LLC's properly. You want to listen to people that you've submitted your script to. Maybe they have some good suggestions. Maybe they're full of crap. The rules of discernment still apply.

"You've got to have the skills to identify who's giving you good advice and who's just trying to sell themselves to you for a job. That's the real challenge."

~ Armen Kaprelian

HONING YOUR CRAFT

Unlike acting or cinematography, or nearly any other craft, directing isn't something that you can just practice on a whim.

Consider the enormous investments of time and energy that musicians, athletes, painters and actors all dedicate to improving their abilities. Directing, on the other hand, is all too often left to a last minute pang of conscience and a dog-eared copy of Directing 101.

Competent directing involves a number of dynamic factors that must, by their very nature, include both environmental, interpersonal, structural and emotional components.

Directing is more guiding than bossing, more cerebral than physical, yet the vast majority of first-time directors do little if anything to actually prepare for the task ahead. Is it any wonder why the overwhelming majority of inaugural projects are so self-indulgently bad?

The first step to becoming a good director is recognizing and then establishing your style. As nearly any successful director will tell you, style doesn't just happen, it must be cultivated. The more unique and individual your particular voice or style is, the more identifiable your work will become.

Some directors are very articulate in their methodology and like to sculpt each performance. David Mamet is rather well known for this and a quick read of his book, *Bambi vs. Godzilla* will give you a scary flash-frame into the mind and motivations of an "A" list director.

Other directors such as Woody Allen and the late Robert Altman were far more passive in their directorial styles. Altman was once asked why he gave so few instructions to his actors. *"I'm looking for something I've never seen,"* he said, *"so how can I tell them what to do?"*

Inside of you there is a voice that is composed of your innermost thoughts and feelings. The directors who have mastered the ability to listen to this voice, when everything around them is clamoring for their attention, are the ones who have made their mark upon the industry.

Simply saying to yourself, *"I will listen to this voice"* will not work; not for you, not for me, not for anyone. The only way to identify the hidden uniqueness within yourself is either through extensive psychoanalysis or focused training and guidance. Personally, I prefer the latter.

If you're serious about the craft of directing there is the unparalleled level of experience that working alongside a recognized professional brings. Formal internships and the training methodology employed by the DGA (Directors Guild of America) are proven methods for developing your craft and working toward realistic goals.

Those impatient to express themselves can find competent guidance in working schools such as The Actor's Studio in New York City, or one of my old alma maters, the American Film Institute in Los Angeles. Your nearest IFP office also has a wonderful series designed to develop your directorial skills.

There are a number of excellent workshops designed to bring out the unique voice that exists within us all. Judith Weston's most excellent Acting for Directors workshops in New York and Los Angeles get you inside the actor's mind and allow you to explore their motivations and methods. Judith's workshops and ongoing classes include support for both directors and actors, and actively involve students in the full process from concept to staging full productions.

When the television shows go on hiatus, most working directors head for exotic vacation spots to decompress from the frantic season — but not Guy Magar. He hits the road and travels the world giving his highly popular two-day Action/Cut filmmaking seminars.

If you can't catch his seminar live in New York, Boston, Miami, Chicago, Denver, Austin, San Francisco or L.A., I recommend his intensive home DVD course.

Guy's seminars are a proven resource for learning the nuts and bolts of directing as a profession and easily the best method for developing your chops outside of working your way up through the DGA program — and a hell of a lot faster.

"There is no question that digital is not only the future, but the very present as well. Besides its unimaginable impact on the world of visual effects, its most immediate contribution has been in the democratization of filmmaking at the grassroots, no-budget level.

"In the excitement of its accessibility, digital technology has clouded a basic inalienable truth: it's not the format, it's the storytelling! Regardless of what format you are recording on, the passion of filmmaking will always lie in the wondrous magic of visual storytelling — the all-encompassing craft of the extraordinary process of translating story words to story images — and that is what I fell in love with. It just happened to be on glorious celluloid during my generation." ~ Guy Magar

Directing takes work and simply deciding that you're a director won't cut it. Without a distinctive voice to your work, and the ability to utilize actors as the pallet of your mind, you're merely another wannabe director standing at the back of the industry's longest line.

SHOW ME THE MONEY!

A lot of people might disagree with my putting the budget under the CRAFTSMANSHIP chapter heading but anyone who's been throughout the process will be glad to tell you that a good budget is a thing of beauty. It's not just numbers on paper, but rather the numerical expression of your vision.

A decent script with a funky budget has less chance of getting made than a mediocre script with an outstanding budget. Put a good script together with a great budget and you've got a true formula for success. Good budgets instill a sense of reliability and confidence in those silly enough to invest in your little venture.

Forget for a moment that you're focused on making a movie. For whatever misguided motives have caused you to undertake this venture, there are a few very solid realities that you need to address.

Moviemaking is an industrial process. It creates a product that will hopefully make money. That is the object. If you have another objective then you are a liability to everyone who you try to con into working on your venture.

I call it a con, because that's what moviemaking without a profit motive is. You're conning people to believe that you're going to take care of them and that their life will be better if they help you make your movie.

So let's forget that the end product is a movie; let's say that you want to make a parachute. You're positive that you want to become known as a famous parachute maker. OK, fine. Have you ever actually parachuted, or have you come to your conclusion because you like to watch parachuting?

Makes sense that you might want to take a few jumps, maybe even learn to fold and pack your own chute — but who has the time these days?

With a red-hot script and a realistic budget in hand you'll have the essential tools you need to go out and start raising money. Unfortunately, a good script is in many ways easier to generate than a good budget.

At the point at which you start to solicit money for your movie, you become a business and as such, should start acting accordingly. Get yourself some legal representation.

I know it sounds dreary and expensive, but there are numerous alternatives such as Volunteer Lawyers for the Arts and the many guild and professional organizations that have legal counselors who sometimes help the occasional loose cannon. Then there's the actual budget. Imagine that you've taken off your director's hat (budgeting for what you want) and put on your Unit Production Manager (UPM) hat (budgeting for what you need).

At this stage, the budget's primary job isn't necessarily to indicate where every penny is going, but rather to give your potential investors the reassurance that you actually have a firm grasp of the production process. There it is for them to see. Your understanding of the whole process, laid out in black and white. The bottom line is obviously very important, but how you arrived at that figure is perhaps even more important.

Since the budget is such an integral and necessary element of production you might want to hire out this process if no one in your immediate production entourage has the aptitude. Don't feel bad. Many right-brained individuals have a hard time with the budgeting process.

The important thing is to have someone who will keep you focused on it through the entire production process. Small extravagances at the beginning can snowball into painful overages by the time you hit editing. The result could be, and often is, a drastic reduction in the amount of resources left to print the video to film.

Perhaps the most common method of creating a budget is by templating. Essentially you beg, borrow or steal the most relevant current budget you can find and make the seemingly appropriate changes.

The problem here is that movies are as different as people are and when you generalize a budget you are essentially "vanilla-izing" your entire project. Add to it that it's a lie, not an auspicious start for a project that'll need all the good karma it can muster.

When you finally get your budget worked out, give it to someone who's done this before just to make sure you haven't missed anything. Numbers are funny things. Commas sometimes look like periods and the next thing you know you're trying to explain why the video-to-film transfer budget is only $5.00. Little mistakes like that not only make you look careless but incompetent.

A much safer and intelligent way to create a budget is to get some good budgeting software like *Turbo Budget* or *Movie Magic Budgeting*, and a copy of Michael Wiese's book *Film and Video Budgets*. It has a wide selection of samples from various production scenarios ranging from feature film productions all the way to "film school chutzpah." It also breaks down the cost per day of every job description in both standard and nonstandard productions as well as supplying you with a comprehensive list of industry standard budget codes.

THE PRODUCER

The Writer, the Director, and the Producer are essentially the trifecta of production.

The function of a writer is so well defined that generally, if someone calls themselves a writer, and they've written anything, you can pretty much consider them a writer.

Directors are a bit more nebulous bunch. Their job is basically to be the cheerleader prior to production, the captain of the ship during production and the janitor in post-production. If someone is foolish enough to want to be a director, let'em have at it I say. Unless they are a real horse's ass, they can't really do that much damage.

The producer however, is much harder to define. Not because the job itself is obscure, but rather because it is a term that is so misrepresented.

Producing is a craft, every bit as demanding and rewarding as any other job in the manufacturing process. There are thousands of people in this industry who call themselves producers. More often than not, they are line producers or production executives.

There's nothing at all wrong with those jobs because they are critically important to getting the movie made. The problem arises when a moviemaker thinks they've got a "producer" and they don't.

Generally speaking, producers who work for a company and get a paycheck every week, regardless of the success or quality of their work are Production Executives. They occasionally call themselves producers but it is usually within the context of the greater production company.

It's a 100 degrees in central Texas. We've just hiked a couple miles up the second largest rock face in the world as Brad lights up a stogie.

Producers all seem to have an extra helping of personality, are all fantastic problem solvers and are all above average intelligence. I have never met an uneducated producer nor have I have met a successful producer that wasn't reading all the time. Scripts, books, treatments, cereal boxes; real producers read a lot.

In addition to having a lengthy string of successes, Brad Wyman is one of my favorite people. I have had the pleasure of working on a number of his projects over the years, so it is with great pleasure that I include this "one cigar" long interview with a man I consider to be a Hollywood producer in the truest sense of the word.

WHAT DOES IT TAKE TO BE A PRODUCER?

INTERVIEW WITH BRAD WYMAN

It doesn't really matter if you're shooting film or digital, the role of a producer is still the same. In a way its a good thing because I'll never get outdated.

If you were to ask any five people, in the industry or in film school, what a director or what a DP is and they'll probably all give you the same answer. You ask the same people what a producer is, chances are that they'll give you five different answers. The word producer is nebulous.

If I can teach one thing to anybody it is that there are three rules to being a producer.

1 Get the money.

2 Never forget to get the money.

3 Always remember to never forget to get the money.

That's the job. People ask if putting the crew together, casting, scripting changes, securing locations and permits and gear isn't the job. It is, along with marketing and distribution and making the deals, but none of that counts for anything if you don't get the money. That is why there are people like me. Can you raise the money for our movie?

There are plenty of Line Producers who run the actual production, but they don't have a job unless someone gets the money.

What is different now in the digital age is that you don't need to get as much money. In the old days the producer's job was based on the relationships that he had with studios. They were your banks and they financed your movies. Now, you can make a movie for a dollar ninety-five, if you know how.

A producer in the digital age can be very savvy. They can come up with nine characters in twelve locations and have a friend with FinalCutPro and another who knows how to use a camera, and they can make a picture. You could make Breakfast Club today for nothing. You and I just got back from Sundance, how many movies did we see that were made on credit cards?

HOW DOES DIGITAL AFFECT THE BOX OFFICE?

One of the movies that you and I made last year is an exquisite little project called Look. Even the concept within the movie was that no one was in it because it was all based on the reality POV of surveillance cameras.

It's a great movie, everyone who sees it loves it, but we're having trouble finding it a home because we went with good actors who were right for the rolls rather than well-known actors. Obviously, if you can get a big name attached to your movie, it will be easier to raise the money. We are however, working in an industry dominated by event pictures. You need big stars to make 100-million dollar event movies.

It still comes down to a good story, well told, and no amount of technology or innovation can change that. We're in a business that makes a product.

There are some very intriguing and innovative production methods being developed like some of the movies that you've been working on lately. Features like Sky Captain where they throw up a green screen and pull in top names for a day or two. Until the studios get behind the methodology, it will remain in the fringe of the industry. Of course there is a lot of opportunity in the fringe as we both know.

WHERE DO YOU SEE THE PLETHORA OF NEW DISTRIBUTION MECHANISMS LEADING US?

We've completely empowered the filmmaker now. Before digital the only way to get a movie made was to graduate from USC Film School, then sneak onto a lot and pitch your 30-million-dollar movie.

Now you have your own camera; you can edit everything from your computer and then score your entire movie with something like Apple's Garage Band *and then post your trailers on YouTube, DailyMotion or any of half a dozen internet movie sites. Arguably, digital distribution is still in its infancy. It is still sequestered to the computer and hasn't migrated to theaters in any significant numbers yet.*

One of the things that I'm currently working on is a system where an on-line catalogue of content can be beamed into home televisions, telephones, theaters, as free, commercial sponsored or pay-per-view programming. Regardless of the nature of the content, it should have the opportunity to play anywhere.

With appropriate controls and pricing there isn't any reason you shouldn't be able to watch the opening night of a fifty-million-dollar studio feature on your home theatre system.

I seriously doubt that anyone is arrogant enough to think that the only place our movies are going to be watched is in theaters.

I think that we're hoping that the new channels of distribution allow content to be viewed in a wide range of venues. From the finest theaters to the hippest handheld devices; all without the gatekeepers saying that you need 90 million in P&A (Promotion and Advertising) to put it out there.

The writing is on the wall as to where this all will go. Just look at music and the impact that the MPEG compressors had on that industry. It went through some very strange manifestations with a lot of discontinuities, but in the end, you'd be hard pressed to find a young person that isn't quite literally attached to their iPod.

The file sizes for a hundred-minute movie are still a bit cumbersome, but give it a few months, or weeks as it seems. The studios are always the last to figure it out. I'll never forget our good friend Jack Valenti's (former head of the MPAA) quote when the Sony BetaMax came out back in 1976. He called it the "Boston Strangler of the motion picture industry."

The iPod showed us that the vast majority of people would much rather buy a song for 99 cents from a well designed, cross-platform vender than bother with the file swapping and conversions of acquiring it illegally. I'm sure there are much better protections for a 90-minute file than were available back in the early Napster days.

WHAT IS THE FUTURE OF PERSONAL MEDIA DEVICES?

Perhaps one of the biggest opportunities in media distribution is with regard to personal media devices. The iPhone is a great example of this. The tools we use to communicate are merging with the mechanisms for entertainment. To some extent, communications is a form of entertainment so it only makes sense to develop tools that merge and combine previously disparate devices.

Whether we are projecting it onto screens, down linking it to our media rooms, watching it on our phones or bouncing it off of our corneas, there is a growing segment of the population that wants to be connected all the time. Media will become like water; you'll be able to turn it on anywhere. Like water or power or gas, media is the next utility. What started out as "internet hot spots" will become a media blanket that wraps the civilized world. How you will be charged for it is the big question.

WHAT DO YOU LOOK FOR IN A DIRECTOR?

I start a lot of first-time filmmakers and generally only use filmmakers that have written screenplays. When I read the script I ask myself, could I direct the movie? Now, I can't direct and have no urge to ever do so, but if after reading the script, it is so clear to me that I could direct it, then I figure that the writer/director put it on paper succinctly enough that the transposition to film or pixels is a safe bet.

Luckily I've been right more than I've been wrong: Matthew Bright, Patty Jenkins, Adam Rifkin, Steve Buscemi, there's a long list of first-time filmmakers that I've started but they all had scripts that were so clear that they made me feel like I could direct that.

Usually those kind of people didn't just get off the bus from Peoria. They've worked on set, they've gripped and gaffed and worked as PAs and actors and camera loaders. I don't think I've ever read anything that was really on the mark and makable that was written by someone who didn't have some sort of previous experience in the industry.

HOW IMPORTANT ARE FESTIVALS?

As an independent filmmaker, making independent films you want a forum to show your work in an environment where the current industry distribution system is huddled and in a buying mood. The festivals have made an industry off of showing movies that would otherwise not be seen.

Cable has helped quite a bit in getting some of the more commercial ones seen but the diversity of films, the wide range of topics and styles, you really don't get that anywhere but at the festivals.

The same dump truck full of money that the studios formerly spread out over a dozen or so movie projects is now being split between a few franchises.

Festivals have become the primary markets and as studios make less and less product the biggest festivals like Toronto, Sundance, Berlin and Cannes become even more important.

The unfortunate thing is that festivals are becoming as snobby and exclusionary as the studios. A few years ago we were trying to choose which festival to screen at, now, we feel lucky to get into any of the big six. But then, I guess that's why they call it show business and not show hobby.

We're in the business of making movies that will eventually make money. My movies all need to make money or I'm going to have a real problem going out and raising money for my next project.

With that, Brad's cigar went out. He played with it for a few seconds and then crushed it on a rock.

Brad and his contemporaries represent the classic Hollywood producer that we all want to have fall in love with our project and whisk us away on an unlimited budget.

Well, lighten up on the *Lunesta*, folks, because the odds are against you. The vast bulk of motion pictures are made by a handful of mini-major studios.

While the paths and projects of classic Producers and studios often cross, it is companies like DreamWorks, Lions Gate and New Line Cinema that are the true movie factories.

Unlike conventional producer-driven productions, the mini-majors have an army of battle-hardened, business-savvy professionals that collectively manufacture hit movies on a daily basis.

As an independent moviemaker, the most important person in the mini-major corporate structure is the executive in charge of Production, generally known by the unassuming title of VP or Senior VP of Production.

In addition to providing the inertia necessary to keep your project moving forward, they can keep you from stepping on the myriad of land mines that very often cripple new filmmakers.

THE BIG POV

Few, if any, studios big or small can match the ongoing success of Bob Shaye's, New Line Cinema. As one of the most prolific and profitable film studios in the world, New Line is responsible for a significant number of the movies that you've seen in your life.

INTERVIEW WITH DANA BELCASTRO

I asked my friend Dana Belcastro, who is a Senior Vice President of Production at New Line Cinema, for her ground level take on the state of the industry with regard to digital production.

Studios have been slow to come to the digital table; and that's because studios are like big, fat luxury liners, we can't change course quickly or easily.

Digital for features was, for a long time, looked at with a combination of fear and suspicion, partly because we hate change, partly because we're naturally cheap and partly because, let's face it, the digital image wasn't really up to snuff.

If you're going to spend $20 million for an actor's gorgeous face, it better look gorgeous. Studio execs love to analyze costs, and with regard to digital camera systems, the differentials couldn't easily be defined at first.

The average feature costs between $60M and $80M to produce and release costs are about the same — the colossal risk we take with every picture necessarily makes us conservative. So when something new comes around, we don't really want to hear about it.

However, in the last few years a couple of repurposed ENG cameras (the VariCam the Sony F-900) and a couple of digital

Dana Belcastro on the set of a block-buster in the making.

cameras specifically designed for features (the Viper, the Panavision Genesis) have been used by studios with some success.

WHAT EFFECT HAS THIS HAD ON HOW YOU MAKE MOVIES?

So now we all have to start taking it seriously. Here's what I've discovered so far:

On the positive side:

- *You're loading 50-minute tapes as opposed to 10-minute film mags. This is especially great for comedies when you're running to capture comedic magic and don't want to have to cut and lose momentum.*

-   You know exactly what you have at the end of the day, no nail-biting until the next day to see if you've got focus problems, etc. The DP can experiment with color correction on set, which potentially saves time and money in the DI process. This is especially helpful when shooting in remote locations where film dailies can't be available quickly.

-   The cost for a camera like the Genesis, which is about three times higher than the usual 35mm package, is more or less balanced out by savings in film and lab and probably some labor and equipment (though this is still up for debate).

On the negative side:

-   Those 50-minute loads encourage directors to just keep rolling. You end up with a huge amount of film which may require additional hard drives and labor ($$) in post to deal with it all.

-   The quality of the image is different from film (which everyone finally seems to be acknowledging), it's more unforgiving on skin tones, pores, hair follicles — extreme close-ups on beautiful actors can be a little icky — really, no one needs to see any of that!

-   The requirement of the "Black Tent" where both DP and director have a tendency to hide out can lose you time and direct communication with talent and crew.

Some of this is quantifiable and some of this is not.

HOW DOES THIS IMPACT YOUR PRODUCTION MODEL?

When the Avid editing system first came around, the complaint from the studios was that it offered a director infinite choices, and therefore would cost us time and money. This may have been true at first, but once everyone got a grip on how it all worked and how it fit into the average post schedule, it's become a huge advantage and a time-saver.

The same panic occurred when the DI (Digital Intermediate) technology first became available. David Fincher famously spent months tweaking every frame of Panic Room and every studio exec in Los Angeles accordingly flipped out. Now, of course, it's normal operating procedure: the costs are more or less set and it takes an average of about two weeks to get through the process. Everybody's happy.

Similar fears arise when considering digital technology when applied to features. At this point, it seems that the additional costs and savings are more or less a wash.

Most of the practical matters will be solved soon enough: Make-up and hair will come up with strategies to protect the actors so they don't look like Barbie dolls. Panavision will figure out how to reduce the weight of the VTR system on the Genesis so it can go untethered and be easily used on a Steadicam rig: all this stuff will be solved with time and experience.

Which kind of brings us to the point. If it doesn't cost significantly more or less, and the only real impact is aesthetic, then why should we bother?

GOOD POINT.

Until the distribution world makes us, why should we go out on a limb? So we can pay some high-priced DP to learn the system on our dime? Great. He becomes more marketable, we have a funky-looking negative, which in the end is going to get fixed in the DI anyway.

WHAT IS THE SOLUTION?

Here's what I've finally come to believe: if we don't take the risk and responsibility now, if we don't figure out how to make it better now, if we don't give craftsmen time and experience to make it a viable, efficient system now, well, then we'll be caught with our pants down come the revolution. The technology is here and it will be dominant within ten years.

So while I'm probably not going to use a digital camera system on my next $100M movie, I'll certainly give it a shot on something more in the $20M to $30M range. Sure it's a little scary and might get a bit ugly, but so is making a film, any film; so why not get in step with what independents have realized for years? Take the risk, have some fun — it's only a movie.

THE STUDIO JUGGERNAUT

There seems to be a prevailing mindset in the independent film community that the studios are the enemy; they are not. It has been my experience that some of the sharpest minds and most genuinely warm people in the business work for them.

The studio system has given us some of the industry's greatest talents on both sides of the lens and created such a mythos out of our little manufacturing process that you'd be hard pressed to find anyone, anywhere in the world, who wouldn't love to be part of it ... And yet even I can't help taking an occasional poke or two at such a plodding beast.

Many well-known filmmakers first started working in this industry using short ends that were left over from studio productions. When I first started experimenting with using personal computers in motion picture production, the 75-year-old head of Universal Studios gave me an office on the lot just so they could keep the future in sight.

A few years ago Warner Brothers was gracious enough to let us shoot Faye Dunaway's HiDef movie *Yellow Bird* on their back lot. For them it was a chance to see how the new technologies integrated into cinematic studio methodologies.

There is a tendency to hold the studios accountable for every problem a filmmaker encounters. Lack of support, lack of funding, lack of resource, lack of distribution — this misperception stems from a basic misunderstanding of the way the current studio system works.

Studios do not make movies anymore. They make deals, and serve as a hub for numerous "mini-majors" who generally further subcontract to various production companies (my own PixelMonger is one), who then hire on freelancers to augment their own in-house staff. In the big five major studios, there are probably less than a few thousand actual employees, but they in turn support millions of people as their connections expand.

In a way, the movie studios are the ultimate metaphor for the Internet. A central hub connecting smaller, more mobile versions of itself who in turn rely on numerous smaller independent companies to actually create the content. Problem is, new distribution mechanisms start at the bottom and don't need the top. The feet simply disconnect from the rest of the body and walk away.

The new generation of studios will be online. More a group of people who agree upon a common set of digital standards than a physical environment. The new studio is unencumbered by the need to maintain a physical property and the obligatory staff of lawyers and MBAs.

I shoot a lot of elements for movies and even entire television shows on chroma key sound stages. This means that substantial amount of environments and virtual set pieces needed to be made.

All but two of the fifteen people who comprised my post-production crew live in either Spain, France, Italy or the UK, and few of us have ever met personally.

We use a private area of my PixelMonger website to exchange data sets and coordinate our designs. By standardizing our computer platform and applications we only need to post a single, low-resolution reference frame and FTP the application's setup file.

Since we do all of the rendering here in L.A., the actual data transfers are quite small.

We are almost continually in production on shows for Discovery Channel, History Channel and HBO. Our production crews are in Lithuania, Greece and the UK. We communicate daily via the internet, and coordinate the hundreds of plates and elements that will comprise these ambitious projects.

Because of its global proximity, virtual studios are able to resource a high-density mix of production people and creatives. With increased efficiency comes increased economy.

The ability to collaborate globally has opened the very process of production up to the point where nearly every significant motion picture in the last several years has elements that were created outside the gates of Hollywood, a trend that will only escalate.

DUELING FOR HEMISPHERES

One of the most powerful tools of the digital moviemaker is computer graphics. What was once the esoteric macrocosm of geeks and nerds has been brought down to affordable, mortal levels. You would be hard-pressed to find a movie that didn't have a little pixel dust on it.

There are essentially two distinct worlds in motion-graphic post-production, and depending on which side of your brain is more active, you'll generally develop an affinity for 2D or 3D.

Two-dimensional (2D) artistry basically includes various combinations of ROTOSCOPING, RETOUCHING and COMPOSITING.

ROTOSCOPING is the process of frame-by-frame manipulation of an image, to add or eliminate a graphic component. Year after year, one of the most often requested visual effects we perform is the removal of blemishes from famous faces. As you can imagine, it is a process that is not taken lightly.

RETOUCHING involves a number of graphic tricks that essentially enhance the look of the image. Very often this includes removing wires and gear used to suspend and protect actors and stunt people, as well as removing the inevitable scratch or two that has long been the bane of this industry.

COMPOSITING involves combining two or more images and can be as simple as placing the weatherman over his animated maps or as complex as scenes with numerous layers and graphic elements.

We recently re-created the *Battle of Actium* for the Discovery Channel. The battle took place off the coast of Greece in 31 B.C. between the navies of Antony and Octavian.

The master shot included seven hundred plus ships, each with five hundred rowers manning huge wooden oars while several hundred little CG Legionaries hurled arrows, spears and flaming balls of fire at each other. The shot required almost two thousand layers containing more than a quarter million elements.

Three-dimensional (3D) methodology includes creating virtual sets and characters as well as a growing number of effects such as digital explosions, clouds and atmosphere.

VIRTUAL SETS were first introduced in the late eighties and are basically sets that are built in a computer, into which your live characters can be composited. What started out as a novel way to cut production expenses has turned into an increasingly popular production alternative.

The inevitable follow up to virtual sets was, of course, VIRTUAL ACTORS. Perhaps the most famous virtual actors to date are the dinosaurs in *Jurassic Park*, but there have been quite literally thousands of digital actors walk across our screens since then.

From the Captain and crew of the *Titanic* in James Cameron's epic tale to the legions of warriors in George Lucas' latest *Star Wars* installment, the number of virtual actors continues to expand as they continue to get closer and closer to the camera.

Hundreds of sword wielding CG Romans battle it out aboard CG ships in the Battle of Actium.

The more sophisticated digital technology becomes, the more it blurs the lines between what we perceive as real and what is real.

And what would a blockbuster be without explosions? Digital effects such as explosions, fog, rain and smoke are very often grouped into a category called VOLUMETRICS because they take up true 3D space rather than being represented as a flat surface.

As the computer's camera moves into a volumetric effect such as a cloud of smoke, the scene will darken progressively and visibility will decrease until the camera comes out the other side.

The ever-expanding digital tool set is giving filmmakers with limited resources the ability to compete with big budget productions. When partnered with the new generation of cinematic quality digital cameras, the true power of digital produciton is unleashed.

I'll deal with some specific computer methodologies in the HACKS chapter. Till then...

AUDIO

People get a little over half of their information about the world around them from their eyes. A classic study done at Yale revealed that people are influenced 55% visually (what they see), 38% vocally (the content of what they hear), and 7% verbally (how things are said).

Of course then you open the whole can of worms about the method of projection, the type of audience and which modality they are using to take it all in. Some people are more visual, or acoustic, or kinetic in how they perceive things, but regardless of how you break it down, sound is one the most dependable generators of emotion filmmakers have in their quiver.

Since all camcorders have built-in microphones, the first person to be eliminated from the low-budget production is all too often the soundman. Oops. The less experience you have in capturing high-quality images, the more imperative it is to have a competent sound man and create an environment that is conducive to recording a good audio signal.

First thing to take into consideration is the camera's built-in microphone. *Do not use it!* Even if you are a lone gunman, out there shooting away on your own, don't even think about it. The first rule in recording sound is to get as close to the source as you can without getting into the camera's frame.

If you're a one-man-band and don't have a soundman to hold the boom, get yourself the best "mini shotgun" microphone you can afford.

Attach it to your camera with a mount that has at least a little isolation to it, then get a "dead kitty" windscreen to cover the business end and leave it there.

Like every other auto function on your camcorder, the automatic volume control should be super-glued in the off position.

Generally, the farther away the microphone is from the sound source, the more noise (ambient sound) it will pick up. The reason that you occasionally see boom mikes in pictures and television shows is not because these people are clumsy, but rather because they are so focused on getting the best sound possible that they often "push the frame" in an attempt to get the mike as close as possible.

The second rule in recording sound is to record your source as loudly as possible without over-modulating. You can always turn it down in post but when you try to turn the volume up, you'll also be turning up any ambient noise that was recorded.

One of the best ways to get good, dependable sound in a "lone gun-man" environment is with lavaliere mikes. These tiny mikes can be hidden in clothes, behind ties and even in hair. Since they're close to the source they generally capture a fairly good signal. They can be hooked to a transmitter for wireless transmission to a receiver attached to the camera.

When you're behind the camera you've got enough to worry about without the added demands of acquiring a good audio signal. For this reason a soundman is perhaps a most necessary addition to the small film crew.

The tiny meters and dials of the camcorder are not a viable alternative to accurate sound acquisition. This is doubly important if you're using a camera that doesn't allow for manual operation of the audio feed. It is for this reason that many, if not most, small format video productions use an external DAT recorder.

When using an external recorder, be sure to slate each shot with a good crisp snap so that you can line everything up in post.

Most experienced soundmen will tell you that once you set the level for a take, don't touch it until the take is over. The other thing they'll tell you is never leave a location without getting at least a minute of "room tone." This is merely a sample of the environment that the editor can use to "glue" performances together with at a later date.

Just as the environment shapes light, it also shapes sound. A set or location with flat, hard walls will bounce the sound around giving the location a "hot" or "live" sound, while a location with soft furniture and objects on the wall will give a softer, less echoic (dead) sound.

One of the most serious drawbacks to tiny HDV format is its inability to record a true "SMPTE" time code. I know the numbers on the camera's little LCD screen move like time code, but the unfortunate reality is that they're only a relative numeric reference that doesn't transpose.

While this problem is endemic and affects nearly every aspect of post-production, I'm putting it here under the AUDIO heading because this is where it causes the bulk of its problems and also where the majority of the solutions lie.

Many people use an electronic Time Coded Slate (with external time code generator) plugged directly into a DAT recorder. A snap of the slate will then give a good visual reference on the video image so the time code can be matched in post. It is very helpful if the soundman runs a channel of audio back to the camera to use as reference. This is especially useful if you're going to transfer to a more robust format for your on-line edit.

Although DAT has been a welcome addition to the set since its intro-duction, today's cameras and recording systems have such good audio capabilities built in that many people simply record the sound along with the image. There is a common argument against this practice stating that if the tape is damaged that you'll loose your audio. The obvious assumption seems to be that if the tape is damaged, you won't need the audio anyway.

EDITING

In the late 1980s we started seeing the first wave of non-linear editing systems. EditDroid, LightWorks, Avid and others started attacking the status quo. For a hundred years, editors had been handling their film with such unchanging mechanical tools as the Steenbeck, the Moviola, and the Kem. Tons of equipment, some of it fifty years old or more, constantly churning out Hollywood's gross national product. Most, if not all, saw this digital invasion as an affront to the craft of editing.

The vast majority of the old school of editors never did adapt and slowly slipped into retirement as a new generation of faster, more efficient editors took over the industry. In the end, it may be the director who tells the story, but it's the editor who translates it. The old guard, with their lifetimes of "hands-on" craft experience, were being replaced in an instant by brash young film students with several years of theory under their belts. The industry itself buckled under the blow as the tide of independent films began to swell.

The laws of film elitism require that every self-professed film lover proclaim the virtues of low-budget, independent cinema while bemoaning the dismal plight of the big-budget, studio blockbust-ers. Well, big budget or small, there is no other single element of the production process that so codifies the final product as being good or bad as editing.

Good editing can elevate mediocre directing and barely competent cinematography far beyond its humble birthright. Of course it also works the other way around.

Sometimes it seems as though I've owned and used every major non-linear edit system that there ever was, including a prototype laserdisc based EditDroid (1987), PC-based EMC2 (1989), 486-based LightWorks (1991), Adobe Premiere/CineWaveHD, Macintosh-based Avid Media Composer (early 1990s), and the most bulletproof system that I've ever owned, the Media100.

If you've read either of the first two editions of this book, you know I wasn't a big fan of Apple's FinalCut edit software. The install was clunky, the interface was buggy and the performance was downright undependable.

More than twenty projects later, I'm a fan; in fact it is all that I use. It took the G5 to give it enough power and an entirely updated operating system to give it enough speed, but FinalCutPro is finally production grade and it rocks. Of the last ten feature motion pictures that I have worked on, eight of them were edited on FinalCut.

WHERE TO START?

There are certain aspects of conventional production methodology that don't really change because of innovation. One such thing is "Tone & Bars" in video and the counter in film.

Black at 00:58:00:00, then Bars and Tone from 00:58:30:00 to 00:59:30:00, then black to 00:59:40:00, then slate (includes the film's name, the production company and date; later you'll come back and add the running time) to 00:59:50:00 where you'll insert your count-down numbers and a beep at the top of each second from 10 to 2. At the end of the "2" you go black until 01:00:00:00 (one hour) where the program begins.

Any creativity or liberties taken at this point will not only screw up every professional that comes in contact with your movie but it will also make you look like a clueless dork.

Fade up from black....

SCORING YOUR EPIC

So you finally got to the end of your edit and now it's time to add the score. This is how you not-so-subliminally tell the audience how you want them to feel about scenes and characters.

The thematic underscore creates mood and texture. A scene underscored with violins and trumpets can cause emotions to swell with majestic expressiveness while a lone oboe can escort your audience into an almost cathartic empathy with your characters.

In the standard Hollywood fare all too often we see every gesture and nuance underscored with dramatic themes. The audience never gets a chance to make up their own minds or breathe.

On the other end of the scale is the small budget production that is forced to use canned music. Often the emotion and theme don't match or the timing is off.

There are a lot of jobs in production where you can fake it to some extent and still end up with a good movie. This is not one of them.

Music is so integrated into nearly everything we do that it is always better to have no scoring at all than to have bad scoring. If you can't do it correctly, it might be better not to do it at all.

With most projects there is a budget for the scoring, but it is all-too-often the first thing to get nicked when production goes over.

For those who might be starting out on their first couple productions, you might consider buying a library resource and then shaping the tempo of your story to it.

In these instances it is often better to lay an audio reference track down and edit the scene to it. As blasphemous as this may sound, a good sound track has a pacing to it that is based on thousands of years of refinement.

By editing your scene to that evolving thematic correlate, your scene takes on a tempo and pace that not only merges it with the musical underscore but also conforms it to an established tempo.

Lastly; a tip from working directors around the world. Write a song or little theme for your movie and make sure it gets into the credit roll at the end. ASCAP (American Society of Composers, Authors and Publishers) and BMI (Broadcast Music, Inc.) are not-for-profit performing rights organizations which license and collect royalties for performance of its members. They also track sales and screenings of your movie far better than the DGA or any motion picture organization ever could. This is the only way that I know of to track your movie's true performace.

FESTIVAL STRATEGY

Once you've made your masterpiece, you need to get it seen by people who will buy it. Plain and simple. It took me nearly 200 film festivals to figure out my strategy, and I'm giving it to you here.

Every festival has a personality and the trick to getting your film in a festival is picking the one that most closely matches the persona of your movie. We all want to be in Sundance and Cannes, but it just isn't going to happen; however there are back doors.

All of the *Big 5* major festivals (Cannes, Venice, Berlin, Sundance, and Toronto) have developed alternate venues. While these alternative screenings may not be on the official ballot, they are in the same neighborhood and the buyers are just as anxious to see them as they are the *Official Selections*. Sometimes more-so.

At Cannes, my favorite is *Director's Fortnight*, which is an independent side festival organized by the *French Directors Society*.

While we were still in post on Matt Dillon's directorial debut film *City of Ghosts*, we campaigned heavily to get him in the *Fortnight*. We knew that the *CoG* was not what Cannes was looking for, but as a new director, his movie was a stand-out.

Other good alternative festivals at Cannes are the ever popular *Social Visions, International Critics' Week* and one of my personal favorites, *L'Acid*. The *Marché du Film* actively solicits independent films from a wide swath of American sources and has helped more than a few *Réalisateur de Film Américain* bust their chops on the Croisette.

Want something closer to home? Sundance has turned into a studio outlet but there are a slew of side venues that have filled the void. Top of the list is *SlamDance*, which was formed to pick up the independent banner that Sundance dropped several years ago. I have a picture in one of the Sundance side festivals nearly every year. They always get great response and they always sell.

For moviemakers without a million dollars of P&A, success at festivals is all about real estate.

At this year's Sundance there were a couple guys who walked around at night and projected their movie on the side of buildings. *Brilliant!* I saw pieces of their movie several times, as did hundreds of festival goers I would imagine.

At Lindsay Lohan's Sundance party there were a couple different people who were showing trailers of their projects in very unusual ways. At the risk of sounding like a pervert, the most interesting approach was one where the producers had hired a very buxom young lady to cleverly mount a small video screen between her breasts. Needless to say, there was always a crowd trying to get a "closer look" at this movie's trailer.

Getting in a festival is not necessarily the hardest part. Building the buzz and breaking through the noise and media clutter is what you need to focus on.

Stickers, flyers, postcards and a nice little press kit are all important elements of your on-site promotional campaign. Plaster the town with your propaganda. Be as aggressively promotional as your psyche can handle.Every festival has billboards where filmmakers can put up posters or flyers of their movie. You need to be diligent about this because a more aggressive promotional team will cover you up in a couple hours at *Cannes*; thirty minutes at *Sundance*.

My friend Adam Rifkin is a festival Veteran, and having worked on a number of his movies, I can assure you that there are few who can give you better advice.

"If and when you get your independent movie into a festival, more important than having the audience like it, is having the buyers there to see how much the audience likes it. Festivals are your best chance to sell your movie, so it only makes sense to get your movie into the festivals that the buyers go to.

"Getting your movie into a festival is only half of it though. Competition is ferocious, and even if you've made a gem, it doesn't stand a chance without some very inventive and persistent promotion. You've got to create a buzz that makes everyone want to see your movie over the other half dozen movies that may be screening simultaneously in other festival locations.

"Ideally you want more than one buyer to get excited about your movie and start a little bidding war. I've seen movies, made for thousands, sell for millions of dollars more than what the filmmakers were hoping for, just because one buyer didn't want to be out-bid by a competitor. It's like that famous Irving Thalberg quote: "A movie never looks as good as when the other fellow wants to buy it."

"There are a number of ways to build "buzz." *The internet is perhaps the fastest and most accessible resource the indie moviemaker has. Quite a few successful movies that got their launch from an inventive viral campaign.*

"Internet campaigns are also helpful in getting your movie into festivals. Trailers, clips, feature-ettes and behind-the-scenes promotional elements can spread like wildfire if you put a little original thought into it. If your trailer gets hundreds of thousands of views on YouTube, and you send that information to the buyers, you're raising awareness that will translate into eyeballs at the festival.

"When you're finally at the festival, you need to maintain a presence. The media clutter at a major festival is enormous and it is very easy to get lost. You show up with all your posters, your stickers, your flyers and promotional materials and pimp your movie like your life depended on it.

"The poster boards fill up fast and your movie's poster can get covered up in a matter of minutes. You need to have a full-time crew out on the street that does noting but keep your poster on the top. As easy as it is for a filmmaker to get sucked into hanging out at the parties and clubs, you've got to maintain your focus and keep actively promoting and campaigning.

"At the recent SunDance/SlamDance festival, we dressed a couple of our PAs up as cavemen and had them out on the street, plastering the town with our HomoErectus posters and flyers. During our "Party Like a Caveman" *premiere party we noticed another event going on across the street at the Egyptian theatre. It was the premiere for* Black Snake Moan *and since a number of the actors were there, a sizable mob of paparazzi and spectators had formed out on the street.*

"We sent our 'cavemen' over to hand out flyers and chat up our movie which was going to premier next. They ended up running through the crowd, throwing fliers in the air, screaming like cavemen and ran right into he chest of a cop: who told them to 'turn around and pick up your mess.' *So now, dressed as cavemen, they had to pick up all the fliers that they had thrown around.*

"It was absolutely humiliating for them and worth every penny that we spent on bailing them out of jail. The buzz that they created helped pack our screening to standing room only. Would it have been packed anyway? Who knows, it sure didn't hurt.

"As it was, a very respectable bidding war ensued and our little caveman comedy is now a National Lampoon Feature." ~ Adam Rifkin

There are lots of other strategies that can help you at festivals but the real key to success comes down to hustle and original ideas.

For more in-depth guidance to building a strong festival strategy, pick up a copy of Chris Gore's book *Film Festival Survival Guide*. He lays out the basics of festival better than any book I've found.

CHAPTER 9

HACKS

Hacks are a form of personal equity and more often than not reflect both the tool kit and the experience of a person that employs them.

As you'll soon see, some of the following hacks revolve around custom gear configurations and computer techniques. There's nothing here that is proprietary or even unusually expensive, just a little different way of putting everything together.

Hacks can be a great shorthand when used correctly, but if taken too far out of context they can quickly become disastrous. With that rather odious disclaimer, I offer up a few of my favorite production hacks. Please, handle with care!

CHROMAKEY

Chromakey is your friend because it releases you from the shackles of reality. There is no other technique that can so drastically increase the scope of your show or so favorably impact the bottom line. Even projects that would not be considered as visual effects productions can benefit greatly from a number of different uses.

One of the most common uses is with regard to pickups. By now it should be *de rigeur* for every production crew to shoot a clean plate or two of a set or location before they wrap out.

When it comes time to shoot that obligatory pick-up or missed line, a little pop-up green screen can save thousands of dollars.

Although the topic of chroma key is encumbered with mismatched bits of outdated information, the practical job of shooting a good element is really quite simple.

- Cloth is better than paper and paint is better than cloth.

- Blue for film, green for digital.

- Blonds on blue, everyone else on green.

- Don't use a bigger screen than you need.

- Costume color conflicts must be taken seriously.

- Pop-up screens can handle most of your needs.

- A little "straw" gel in the backlight works wonders.

- Never let a tracking mark cross the face or hair.

- Turn the camera's detail circuit off.

- Shoot a progressive image whenever possible.

- Get the actor as far away from the screen as possible.

- Match the actor's lighting to the back-plate.

Lighting chroma key was once a difficult task but the newer "digital" colors and the greatly evolved 3-space chroma key software open this powerful process up to anyone with a laptop. Digital green requires far less light than older chroma key green and it lights more evenly. In many cases, available light is all you'll need to pull a great key.

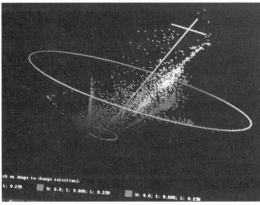

Apple's COLOR software has one of the best 3D colorspace representations in the business.

As one of my favorite gaffers puts it, *"a thermonuclear fusion source with a water vapor diffusion system is the perfect system for lighting chroma key"* (Cloudy day).

3D keyers are far more forgiving than the older 2D systems. You still need to get the screen rather flat, but the increased dynamic range of newer keyers is far more forgiving.

For studio work you'd be hard pressed to beat *Space Lights* for their soft volume and even spread or a couple KinoFlo banks for a more focused spread.

Chroma key software is a long topic; lots of egos, with lots of opinions. Cheapest and easiest chroma key system is Apple's *iMovie* and a copy of GeeThree's *Slick Effects*. At $50, you'll need to spend a whole lot more to get to the next usable keyer.

On the set of director Randal Kleiser's Red Riding Hood. *Space Lights fill the cyc with an even volume of light that makes compositing a whole lot easier.*

Top of the line keyers in daily use at the Billups household include Red Giant's *Primatte*, the Foundry's *Keylight* and *zMatte* by Digital Film Tools. Between my wife and I we pull well over 3,000 mattes a year for movies, commercials and HD television shows.

My wife is an Inferno operator and loves the Autodesk keyers. Whenever I run into a shot that I just can't get to pull correctly, I give it to her. Part of it is that she's just much more talented than I am and part of it is that the Inferno/Combustion keyer is really great.

Tim Sassoon is a Cinemagician. His Santa Monica–based visual effects company blends science and craft to create high-end visual effects for everything from commercials to IMAX. His take:

"The only thing about keying is color correcting the image to make the best possible key without worrying about what it looks like, then using the result as a matte.

"For HDV in post, I'd mention a couple of things. First, if you're going to need a lot of post color correction, I'd recommend shooting with gain up a bit, like +3 db, even if it's bright sunlight, just to noise the image up a bit. That will help keep shadow blocking at bay, and increase the apparent bit depth of the image.

"Another thing is, there's a good chance you'll need to dub the masters to HDCam prior to capture, if one's doing offline, then online conform. Another approach is to capture un-compressed from the get-go, using an HD-SDI or HDMI output, and treat it as if it were coming off an HDCam tape. The advantage of that it using the same hardware codec to decode it as was used to encode, rather than QuickTime's software codec, which can give you a slightly better image."

Another good friend and VFX supervisor, Mike Most adds: *"A composi-tor always tries every possibility before settling on what is usually a combination of techniques to create a quality matte. In almost every case, a 'single solution' matte is not a professional quality matte. Proper mattes almost always require multiple keys of various types and often a degree of rotoscoping before they're as good as they can get.*

"Of course, that's the approach of professional compositors — people who do this for a living. Not editors, cameramen, or producers trying to save money by not using professional compositors."

BIG IRON

A growing number of the movies and shows that I shoot involve vary-ing degrees of green screen. Over the years I've developed a system that allows me to capture the highest quality signal while providing a convenient production and reference station.

The performance window in production technology is moving so fast that if we wait for computers to become ruggedized enough for loca-tion work, the state-of-the-art will have moved on. It is for this reason that it becomes imperative to devise gear, specifically engineered to incorporate current technologies into the production environment.

This current version of my *AppleCart* is based on the Steadicam *LowBoy Dolly* from BackStage Equipment Company in North Hollywood. It was custom fabricated for me by the company's owner. It has spent the majority of its life in trucks and planes, travel-ing between locations and folds into itself for shuttling around on local jobs. It also breaks all the way down to the two side rails and tires for shipping.

Outside the Charlie Chaplin stage at Henson Studios, the newest cart is ready to roll into the oldest stage in Hollywood.

Nearly everything else is speed rail and fittings, which can be pulled from the grip truck on location. Any grip worth his Starbucks can slap this thing together, modify it or dismantle it in just a few minutes.

I've developed a couple of these production carts in various configura-tions, but the majority of them are MacPros with BlackMagic cards and Ciprico RAIDs. They all do 4:4:4 dual-stream HD-SDI and stand up to the wear and tear of real-world production.

1st AC Jeremy Rodgers, preps both my camera and my cart for a day's work at Robert Rodriguez's Troublemaker Studios in Austin, Texas.

One of the great things about having a computer right there next to the camera is that you can use the on-screen diagnostics from your capture application to make sure that you're getting a good bite on the chroma key.

Finish the shoot; load on a copy of After Effects and just hand the whole box off to the artist. Once they finish pulling the key and cutting the garbage mattes, they hand it over to the compositor and they in turn hand it off to the editor.

This industry is so righteously plugged into Moore's Law that you can see the future using simple math.

The instant replay capabilities of direct-to-disk recording are mighty handy when Gary Busey and David Carradine start going at it with clubs.

As someone who has been pushing the limits of digital acquisition and workflow since the very first pixel dust made its way to the big screen, I've come to know two hard facts to be true.

1) If you use the newest, hippest gear, you will always suffer and lose both time and money. Stay away from anything with "-est" at the end of its description *(e.g. newest, latest, coolest).*

2) If you wait for leading edge technology to become ruggedized enough to use in conventional production, you will be three to five years behind the curve.

The secret lies in developing systems using time-tested, grip-friendly gear. I just can't stress the *grip friendly* part enough.

Production methodology is not about automating the process, but rather getting powerful tools in the hands of those

Camera operator Tom McDonald records to tape and hard drive on the set of Closing Escrow.

involved. When all those tools talk to each other, we get some truly amazing results.

As the methodology of digital production becomes more evolved, we'll see more post-production being done during actual production stage. As any banker or money manager can tell you, the shorter the turnaround on the investment, the more business you're going to do.

NLE AS AN ACQUISITION ENVIRONMENT

As you probably surmised, I'm a long-time fan of direct-to-disk recording. Back in the late eighties and early nineties it was a real pain in the ass, but now there are just so many great tools to work with that it has developed into a growing component of production.

My first choice for visual effects work is RAW 4:4:4 @ 4K from a RED, Viper or some other big gun. The reality of production however is that you almost never get your first choice.

Many visual effects shots are done in post, long after the budget has started to atrophy. My second choice is a 2K or high-end HD camera such as the Sony F-23 or the Panasonic HPX3000. Usually we end up with an F-900, and because there are so darn many of them, there is usually a deal to be had somewhere.

If the budget has gone belly-up, and there is no more blood to be squeezed from the stone, I pull out my trusty Canon XLH-1. Since the progressive HD-SDI signal is very high quality and the camera is inexpensive enough to have sitting around collecting dust when I'm off doing something else, it makes an unusually cost-effective alternative to conventional film or HD acquisition.

The author captures an Amazon warrior direct-to-disk.

One of the great things about plugging a camera directly into a computer is that you can use programs like Premiere as an intervolometer to not only capture continuous sequences but time-lapse and stop-motion sequences as well.

In conventional cinematography the intervolometer is a step motor that advances the film a single frame and then triggers the camera to expose it. You've no doubt seen those shots of clouds sailing across the sky (one frame per minute) or flowers blooming (six frames per hour) or buildings being built (four frames per day) or seasons changing (twenty frames per month): all intervolometer. Premiere has a cool little control window that is easy to use and bulletproof — two of my favorite features.

Then there's the stop-motion and puppet motion work such as Tim Burton's *The Nightmare Before Christmas,* which was actually directed by Henry Selick who went on to direct *James and the Giant Peach* and then *Monkeybone* (which my wife did quite a bit of work on). Unlike the time-lapse intervolometer system that takes a frame automatically every *n*th second, the stop motion capabilities of Premiere capture a frame every time you hit the space bar.

Put a fertile mind together with these kinds of tools and something strange is always going to happen. Among my favorites are damn near anything Nick Park *(Wallace and Gromit)* does and of course, the meister of the unusual, Terry Gilliam *(Monty Python, Jabberwocky, Time Bandits, Brazil, Adventures of Baron Munchausen, Brazil, The Fisher King, Brazil, Twelve Monkeys, Brazil, Fear and Loathing in Las Vegas, Twelve Monkeys and, of course... Brazil).*

Don't have a Viper or F-900 or even a Canon XLH-1? No problem: Virtually any digital still camera that has the capability to over-ride the auto functions is capable of winning you an Academy Award for best animated short. I judge a number of film competitions every year and have been seeing quite a few very compelling projects that were done this way.

Not exactly the way you want to work or the way you want to tell your tale? Get over it. Any story ever devised can be told in hundreds of ways. From IMAX film to iPod QuickTimes, it is only about unveiling aspects of persona and environs. Size doesn't matter. Resolution doesn't matter. Length doesn't matter. Budget doesn't matter.

In last year's *Action/Cut Short Film Festival* one of my favorite movies was done with pencil and paper. That my friends is the difference between a movie maker and a wanna-be-famous, gizmo-centric, misguided dreamer: and you know how much I dislike dreamers.

To answer the proverbial question of how much a high-end, cinematic production system costs. One used Sony F828 digital still camera = $200; a used computer with a copy of Adobe Premiere (any version) = $200; and that's it, baby. If you can get $400 together and get your head out of the bubble of mythos that surrounds this industry, you don't have any excuses or limitations.

A $400 system can win you an Academy Award.

SUPERFRAMES

In his self-imposed exile from the Hollywood mainstream, George Lucas has developed a cinematic methodology that many are adapting to varying degrees.

By combining progressive HD acquisition with a powerful suite of digital tools, his talented team of acolytes is defining the future of motion picture production.

We've created numerous shows for both the History

My hard working producer Carolina Pacheco, looking all touristy in the south of Spain.

and Discovery Channels using a variation of George's methodology, and even find ourselves using it on motion pictures from time to time.

We call it *SuperFrames*. In addition to cutting the actual production time by nearly 80%, the cost savings are absolutely enormous.

The majority of the action is shot on chroma key sets with high-end, HD cameras and some sort of disk-based system that records the HD-SDI signal from the camera's Serial Digital port.

For the award-winning History Channel show *El Cid* (which I also wrote and directed), my line producer and I basically traveled around Spain on a very well-organized schedule that took us to the main locations of the Castilian Knight's epic adventures.

Had we shot conventionally, the location fees would have been exorbitant, as would the costs of pulling crew, cast and costume together. We basically shot over 20 locations in under a month for the price of a couple tourist passes and a great vacation in Spain for yours truly and his favorite multi-lingual producer. Ditto Wales, England, France, Italy, Germany, China, Peru and more than a dozen other countries.

The really great thing about traveling around with a still camera is that you look like a tourist. Many of the locations that we shot plates in are simply off limits to production crews. Combining that plate, however, with a thoughtfully composed green screen shot can add thousands of dollars of production value for the price of admission.

This methodology may sound quite simple, but to do it right takes every cinematic chop you've got.

The object is to shoot your locations with a good digital still camera. I use a Sony F828 digital still camera because it has nearly the same gamma as the Sony F-900's HD-SDI signal. It shoots an 8 MegaPixel image so there is a lot of room to pan your HD frame around in.

I generally use either a Canon XL-2 or and XLH-1 for motion elements within the SuperFrame because of their unusually good progressive image. Like the F828, the image cuts very nicely with the F-900, F-950 or Viper footage.

There are a number of pieces of important information that you need to record at each location. Top of the list is lighting. There is no trick of compositing that will match an element to a back plate more than a good lighting.

For years I've had people hold up a white balloon. This not only gives me good idea of the source and fill, but also of the quality of light and how hard and dense to make the shadows. Angle of view is another important piece of information, which rarely, if ever makes it into post.

I've developed a chart specifically for this type of work: *http://www.dsclabs. com/the_billups_vf_x.htm*. The chart's white and black balls give you all the lighting information that the balloon

The balloon tells the story.

does, in addition to color temperature. Other elements give distance to camera, lens and camera angle and a dozen other pieces of information that help compositors create their illusions.

The trick is to shoot your plates cinematically. Get a good establishing shot, then your masters and your reverses. Then come around for your over-the-shoulders, tights, point-of-views and various coverage elements

You might find it invaluable to do a meditative visualization where you sit down in the location and read the scene and imagine what it will look like with the characters standing before you.

How wide do you need to be to get a good master? What interesting angles will give you a greater sense of presence? Is there anything you need to accommodate for? If there are signs, do you have a good texture sample that you can use to roto over it? Do you have a good selection of doors and entrances as well as hallways and routes leading to and from this location?

If you have enough coverage so that your show keeps moving and cutting, the audience will never suspect that you're using plates, much less still images.

The best system seems to be to shoot a plate both with and without a flash. This gives you more exposure options with which you can alter the densities in post. If there is a bright window and you're shooting in a castle with dark stone walls, lock the camera down and shoot a range of exposures so that if the window is blown out in a shot that exposes the room well, you can cut or blend in a window from a darker shot.

John Glen's 1992 epic feature, CHRISTOPHER COLUMBUS paid nearly $100,000 to shoot in this location. We paid $6.

Very often you'll be trying to shoot a location that has a lot of tourists in the frame. If you had a permit you'd be able to block them off or at least regulate their access. But hey, you're shooting bandito style. The trick is to use a long exposure. While a 1/250th of a second exposure might include a dozen tourists, a two-minute exposure will magically give you a clean frame.

In really crowded environments such as train stations or city streets you might need to use exposures as long as five or ten minutes. The trick is to keep everyone moving in the frame. If someone stays in one place too long, walk up next to them and start coughing as if you have the flu. They will invariably give you an odious look and move on begrudgingly. Using this system you'll be able to get amazing plates in some of the most crowded tourist locations in the world.

One of the locations that we shot extensively was the amazing Moorish fortress complex in Granada, Spain called the Alhambra.

The massive complex occupies a hilly terrace and is easily one of the most diverse and majestic locations that I have ever witnessed.

We shot there for three days and during that

Six planes of action added real production value to this shot.

time we came across a BBC production crew that was shooting a rather simple scene in one of the Alhambra's numerous environments. Their budget was the equivalent of $11,000 a day while ours was the equivalent of $12 a day.

When you finally get on your chroma key stage, make sure you have all your plates organized and easily accessible to your crew for reference. It is good to have a couple copies of printouts as well as plates in the computer for a quick composite if needed.

By shooting progressive HD directly to the computer's hard disk and having the back plates loaded for quick and easy reference, you can pre-comp scenes before sending actors back to costume.

While we're on the subject, this methodology is so efficient that you can easily shoot out 20 or more pages in a day.

Make sure your costume and hair and make-up are prepared for the unusually fast pace, otherwise your glorious system of production efficiency will be brought to its knees by a backstage human logjam.

We have shot over two dozen shows this way in nearly every corner of the planet. The cost savings have been enormous and having worked on both of this year's prime-time, non-fiction Emmy winners, it is probably safe to say that the production value is quite respectable.

SUPERFRAME ACTION PLATES

Speaking of which, the overall visual effects process we used for creating the major visual effects sequences in the History Channel's Emmy-winning *Ten Days That Changed America: Massacre at Mystic* involve a process that we call *SuperFrame Action Plates.*

As with the basic SuperFrame technique, it involves creating a massively large environmental plate, into which are placed live action sequences shot in progressive video.

Let's face it, most elements in the background of a scene don't move. There is however the occasional opportunity to ad some movement to the plate such as smoke or a waterfall or a flag waving in the breeze.

Think of the SuperFrame back-plate as a large patchwork quilt. By shooting progressive frames in either SD or HD you can paste patches of motion elements (video) into the back plate composition using programs such as Adobe After Effects or Apple's Motion. Once constructed, the computer software can then perform all the framing movements of a real camera.

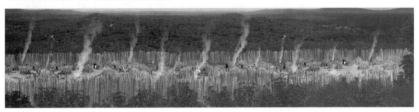

A standard definition television picture is 720 pixels wide while a HD picture is 1920 pixels wide. The SuperFrames that we used for *Massacre at Mystic* were more than 8000 pixels wide, so we had plenty of room to push in, pull out and pan across the image.

In addition to the massive horizontal and vertical size of the SuperFrames there are also the layered components. In much the same way the masters like Botticelli, Bosch, da

1- *Fore-trees*

2- *Fore-fence*

3- *Smoke elements*   5- *BG trees*

4- *Village comp*   6- *Back plate.*

Vinci and Rembrandt used layer upon layer of subtle tint and image to create the illusion of reality, we too use numerous layers to achieve the illusion of depth and dimension.

In a long tracking shot through the Pequot Indian village there are more than two hundred layers of people, structures atmosphere and smoke elements.

The actors were all shot on location on a green-screen that we had set up near the main set. As actors were wrapped off the main set they would be shuttled down to the green-screen where we would shoot them in a number of motion sequences. By making small costume and makeup changes we could get several performances out of each group of characters, thereby expanding on the resources that we would have when we got into post-production.

Certain elements such as the arrows that hit and interacted with different characters were all CG and we merely rotoscoped them in a conventional manner. Since we were dealing with a number of professional actors, we relied on their craft to "sell" the hits and interactions.

VIRTUAL ENVIRONMENTS

3D environments are another popular way to add production value while having the option to control costs involved. Projects such as Kerry Conran's *Sky Captain and the World of Tomorrow* illustrate the power of CG worlds on a shoestring budget.

Kerry basically hunkered down and, over a period of several years, created the environments for his movie. It wasn't until he was very far along with the CG that he began to add the name actors that got him his wide release.

One of the great things about using CG environments is that you can create very compelling worlds in your spare time. I have a project that I've been working on for five years. It has some great performances by great actors including John Glover, Faye Dunaway and the very last on-camera performance of my good friend Marlon Brando.

Since everyone worked for SAG minimum, and everything was shot on a chroma key stage, the costs involved are so minimal that I can afford to work on it anytime there's a few minutes.

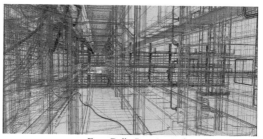

Even Della Rocca's wireframe is impressive.

Unfortunately, that tends to be in airports and airplanes these days. By the time this project is done, it will probably be the first motion picture to be created in airplanes.

As fortunate as I am to have many top quality actors as friends, I'm also fortunate in knowing a large number of very talented artists. For a scene that needed a very *Brazil*-looking, bureaucratic fundamentalism, David Della Rocca whooped up one of my favorite CG environments of all time in Electric Image.

120,000,000 polygons at HD rez took a week to render. But the end result is a scene that would make Terry Gilliam smile.

Truth is, you don't really need to be a good modeler as long as you know one. Libraries such as TurboSquid.com have become the facilitators of the burgeoning *Virtual Hollywood*. As long as you've got an Internet connection and a little room left on your Visa, you're in the big time, baby.

CG CHARACTERS

Even though CG characters are one of my long-time passions, I need to spend my time focused on a number of areas of production, many of which don't have anything to do with computers. As with any software application, you really need to ask yourself if you are a generalist or a specialist.

If you're a specialist, and CG characters are your life's passion, you might want to dig into something substantial like SoftImage XSI, Maya or Studio 3D. If you're a generalist, then e-Frontiere's Poser is just what the doctor ordered.

The very high quality of the models and the numerous content resources make it a great first program for people just getting their feet wet in 3D character animation.

I've used Poser since before it was called Poser, and every version lets the camera get just a little bit closer. We've used it in well over a hundred motion picture and television projects. Resource is the name of the game here and Poser has a larger catalogue of costumes and props than all other 3D applications combined.

It took less than a day to match the costumes of Alexander the Great's army, weapons and all.

We've also built armies for Napoleon, Genghis Khan, Spartacus, King Richard, Ramses, Robert the Bruce, Admiral Nelson, Caesar, Cromwell, King David, Hannibal, Mohammed, Zhukov, Saladin, the Crusades, Troy, World War I and II, the Civil War, the Mayan War and many others, all from the online resources of e-frontier.com and Renderosity.com.

Even up close you've got to look at the ground to see which of the soldiers is computer generated.

REPLICATION

We do so much replication that whenever there is a period show that deals with large numbers of people, the phone invariably rings.

When big-budget, historical event motion pictures crest the production horizon, History Channel, Discovery Channel and maybe a few of the networks will generally develop some sort of ancillary programming.

This kind of thematic co-opting is good for everyone as it raises awareness and generates conversation; and that is one of the secrets to success. Whether initiating a conversation within the viewer's mind or around the water cooler, when people think about it, they talk about it, which motivates other people to want to see it.

Shortly after Oliver Stone started production on his version of *Alexander the Great*, History Channel called and wanted us to work on a show they were doing on the Macedonian leader. A week or two later Discovery called, followed by ABC. After 2,400 years, Alexander the Great was becoming a commodity.

After a few weeks of pre-production we realized that it was insane to do all the

A pop-up and a treadmill can make enourmous army.

shows and passed on the ABC special. Maybe not the best career move, but the show folded a few weeks later when they realized the scope of the story.

At that point we had consulted to all of the Alexander the Great projects and were doing the visual effects and a good deal of cinematography for both of the television specials. The hardest thing was keeping everything from looking the same so we used two different approaches.

Discovery Channel

History Channel

Two different green-screen treadmills, different prop-masters, different costume and make-up, different studios and different cameras.

The reason I bring this all up is that these shows play rather regularly on television so you can see the end results of these hacks.

The easiest and perhaps most powerful *rep* hack is called Paper Doll or Billboarding. There are numerous variations but the basic idea is to cut an image from its background by pulling a chroma key or cutting a matte and then place it in a 3D environment like a billboard.

A very convincing graphic element for 1/1,000th the cost of a staged event.

We've done enormous battle scenes on numerous occasions with two good stunt men and a truck full of costumes.

We shoot combat sequences which we then pull a chroma matte on and sprinkle billboards of that sequence over a battlefield. By starting each clip at a slightly different time you avoid the "chorus line" repetition.

A pop-up greenscreen can turn 9 soldiers into ...

Pop-up green screens are one of the digital movie makers most powerful tools, and for those doing any sort of historical or commercial production, they're indispensable.

... Thousands.

There are a number of good pop-up green screens on the market, and they will all do a good job. The problem with most is that they use a black edging material which invariably crosses the actors and ends up causing many hours of needless rotoscoping. We've tried covering the edges with green tape which works well for a few times but then starts getting glue all over the surface which then attracts dirt.

After years of my "suggestions" falling on deaf ears I ran into Kelly Mondora who is the VP of the F. J. Westcott Company. Not only did she listen to my excessive whining but they immediately added an all green pop-up to their already extensive product line. The color and material that Westcott uses is quite vibrant and tends to light itself. The added bonus of green edges means that we're now done with the comps hours earlier than we were when we had to hand-roto the black edges out of every frame.

The trick is to not use more green than you really need. Simply cover the area that you want to cut into or overlay and then move on to the next shot.

When Oliver Stone was doing his epic Alexander the Great movie we were called in to consult on the construction of the Battle of Gaugamela.

Considered by many historians to be the largest battle ever fought, the Battle of Gaugamela involved more than a million combatants in one place, at one time. Truly freaky numbers for a graphics person.

There is a really cool, really expensive piece of software called *Massive* that basically builds armies or swarms

Alexander looks out over the production vehicles ... er, Alexander looks out over his assembled armies.

of bees or herds of mutant armadillos almost automatically.

You feed in some custom geometry and some motion capture files and it churns out hordes of psychotic robots for *I Robot*, all the armies in *The Lord of the Rings* trilogies, the spectators in *Talladega Nights*, the crowds in Peter Jackson's *King Kong*, and the crazy little penguins in the Academy Award–winning *Happy Feet*.

Massive is truly a great piece of software, but at over $20,000 for a single license, its price is way too massive for a little guy like me. It also starts choking at about 10,000 replicant which wouldn't even take care of a wing of King Durias' army at Gaugamela. Nope, for the really big numbers you've got to use a number of different hacks that, when combined, give the effect that the production company is looking for.

Another, perhaps more sophisticated method of replication is the use of Sprites. The basic concept is to take an image or movie of anything, and then map it into position on a dynamically controlled particle. This technique works equally well for crowds, smoke, swarms, fire and even snowflakes.

The final E=mc² render involved both CG, sprite and bilboard elements which when combined, created a scene of mythic proportions.

For one version of the Battle of Gaugamela we created about fifty little movies of both CG and real actors dressed up as soldiers. We had walking solders, running soldiers (green screen treadmill), fighting solders, solders just sitting around and of course dead soldiers.

In many situations we would simply composite layers of these action loops after we pulled the green screen matte, but for the really big stuff, we pulled out the particles.

Nearly every 3D and most 2D applications have particle systems. They are essentially points in 3-space that are generated from a central point called an Emitter. In addition to being able to create nearly any geometric natural shape, particle systems can also emit polygons, onto which you can map a picture or movie, which is then called a *Sprite*.

By controlling the flow of particles, you can form rather complex clusters that from a distance will do quite well as army formations.

Neither of the show's budgets would accommodate location shots on the Gaugamela Plateau, but we did get great location photos from Oliver's crew that we used as reference to build a CG environment in Vue.

Next we created sprite-based battalions inside geometric shapes called *bounding boxes*. These are basically simple 3D shapes that you can fill with things like butterflies or solders or smoke. Drop a couple hundred bounding boxes on the CG battlefield, hit the render button and go on vacation. A week later a scene pops out that looks like a million bucks — for a whole lot less.

VIRTUAL ACTORS

For the History Channel show we needed to do something with an entirely different look. We've done a lot of CG environments for them over the years that they've always seemed to like so we decided to build a CG army. There are a lot of great 3D programs out there and we have a most of them. Maya and 3D Studio are both great for creating virtual characters in blockbuster motion pictures, but we needed a million soldiers and didn't have a blockbuster budget.

Where Sprites and Billboards are methods of replicating pictures or movies, Flocking involves the replication of actual 3D models. Once you've built your CG soldier it is a relatively simple task to feed it into the flocking module of a dedicated 3D application and have it generate hundreds of anamated variations.

Massive software ($30,000-ish) is the big gun in this category but many far more affordable 3D applications have flocking capabilities either built in or available as a plug-in. Replicating infantry of any era is generally a simple task when compared to cavalry. Horses are not only expensive, they are very time consuming. We've found that by using a flocking system to generate CG horses, and then attaching a billboard of a live action rider to that horse, we can create very high-quality mounted armies.

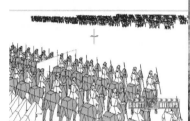

Five horses and similar costumes made this gag into a working shot.

Some of the easier-to-use applications are Flock This ($300-ish), which is a plug-in from Northern Lights Productions for use in Electric Image ($700-ish), and my very most favorite environmental 3D application VUE ($300 ~ $700-ish), which has amazing capabilities built in.

This system works fairly well for anything that you want to use a hundred yards away but for closer work it simply doesn't work unless you have truckloads of cash and a hundred CG artists chained to their workstations.

It is doubtful that you'll have as much need for replication gags as we do, but just understanding the basics can extend your toolset and open your mind to possibilities that you would otherwise dismiss.

The trick to replication, and one that we've found to hold true through hundreds of these shots, is continuity. You want everyone to look different, but not *that* different.

Six extras easily became a thousand Roman slaves by casting for physical similarity.

You'll be making little clusters (pods) of people, and then replicating those clusters many times. If one costume is too unique or one person is wearing something that really stands out (we call it the pink fuzzy-bunny-hat syndrome), then the viewer's eye will notice that costume element in each pod and your gag will be a failure.

Flocking or Spriting, Billboards or comps, CG or flesh-and-blood; replication is a major ingredient of the digital movie maker's tool kit.

3D LOOK IN A 2D WORLD

Every professional desktop motion graphics application has an often hidden capability that can add enormous production value very easily. It is called different things in different applications, but in the most widely used application on both the PC and the Mac (Adobe After Effects) it is simply called "3D Layer."

We had originally hired extras to play the archers in EL CID. Even though "archery" was clearly listed in their resumes, none of them could get off a believable shot. Luckily, my good friend Joe Di Gennaro was manning the camera while I attended to directorial duties. Turns out that in addition to being a great DP, he's also a championship archer.

The object is to import a special 3D camera which in After Effects is done through Layer > New > Camera. This now enables you to move your images in a third axis and allows for three-dimensional movement within the new composition.

Start by creating a very large picture of the ground and then rotate it on the X-axis so that it intersects the back plate at a right angle.

Import a video segment of a person shot on chroma key and line their feet up with the ground plane after pulling their matte.

By stacking your layers in a three-dimensional virtual stage, where the sky is furthest away, and then layering elements progressively closer to the camera, you can create a very dynamic and believable

In addition to serving as DP for a majority of the show, Joe plays all the archers on both sides of the six battle scenes. Our closest guess is that he plays well over 20,000 characters.

perception of depth when the camera moves. It is far more convincing than it would be if the layers were merely composited conventionally on a single plane.

Layering is the key to acheaving a more dynamic presence and greater believability. By building successive layers of background elements you can add great depth to your scene and make a truly interesting world out of a few pictures.

THE GRIP TRUCK AS A TOOL

We often mount a green screen to the side of the grip truck. In addition to not needing to worrying about the wind, it is highly mobile. The sun moves, simply move the truck.

Having tried to shoot a horse on a green-screen treadmill, and having failed miserably, we've resorted to what we like to call the traveling green screen. It basically entails mounting a green screen to the side of the Grip Truck and relies on the skill of the rider to keep the horse in the middle of the screen as the truck moves.

World famous archer/DP, Joe Di Gennaro pans with the action as the horse and rider work to keep pace with the grip truck.

By panning or, even better, dollying with the action, you can get a very high-quality element that can be used in numerous shots. As with hand-to-hand combatants, a very few riders with numerous costume changes can perform miracles.

One of the most overlooked tools in a conventional production is the grip truck itself. That large white surface is perhaps one of the most steady and yet mobile reflectors that you've got.

Imagine that you're doing a truck shot (moving with the actor) while the actor is walking along a sidewalk. Perhaps they are in the shadow of buildings. Buy using the Grip truck to shoot from you are not only bouncing some much needed fill into your scene, but you've also got a very steady platform from which to shoot numerous angles.

LIBRARY FOOTAGE

The success or failure of the vast majority of movies comes down to one thing: Production Value. Unless the viewer can sense a qualitative level of sophistication that meets their expectations, they often won't sit through more than a few minutes of your show.

My ArtBeats collection.

There is no more economical way to expand the production value of your project than with good library footage. My favorite source for a number of years has been the ArtBeats library (www.artbeats.com). If this bit sounds like a commercial, I apologize, it is just that my ass has been saved so many times by this library having just exactly what was needed that I feel as though they deserve special mention.

One thing in particular that sets them apart from all the other libraries is that once you buy the shot or the disk, you own it. Use it for whatever purpose you want for as long as you want, as many times as you want, and no further bookkeeping or payments are due. That may not sound like much but to someone that uses a hundred or more library shots a year, it not only saves a lot of bookkeeping, it saves a lot of money.

Let's say you're shooting a story that takes place in New England or Tokyo or Africa. You, however, live in Iowa. Aside from a big establishing shot, buildings are basically the same everywhere, especially interiors. Once you sell the establishing shot, you can tell just about any story, anywhere.

So you plunk down a couple hundred bucks and buy a nice establishment or two. Not only have you just saved a whole bunch of money but also chances are very good that the shots you just bought are a lot nicer than something you would have gotten on your shoestring budget.

A recent example of how important a good library resource can be happened while shooting the quirky caveman comedy *Homo Erectus*.

As a working cinematographer and visual effects supervisor, my job is to crawl inside the director's head and bring his vision to life. I've crawled into a lot of strange heads in my career, not the least of which is Adam Rifkin's.

While the costumes were little more than faux fur and ultra-suede, the vistas and locations needed to be grand. "Grand" wasn't really a budget option so when it came time to create Adam's vision, I turned my director on to the ArtBeats library. As Adam put it:

"During the production of Homo Erectus, *our epic comedy set in prehistoric times, I needed a series of spectacular aerial shots for our finale. The only problem was, there was nothing epic about our budget. Before resorting to rewriting the entire ending we decided to check out ArtBeats and see if they had anything that was similar to what we were looking for. About 15 seconds into our search not only had we found exactly what we needed, but it was bigger, better and more spectacular than anything we could have shot ourselves. Thanks to ArtBeats, my little caveman movie now looks like a really big caveman movie!"*

Four extras and twenty changes made a very large crowd.

After selecting a few action plates from the ArtBeats web page, we set the camera to an appropriate height and angle, matched the lighting and shot the actors running on a green screen treadmill. One such shot involved a hundred people from several different tribes chasing our main character off of a cliff.

Robert Rodriguez and Quentin Tarantino were gracious enough to take a break from shooting *Grind House* and let me come in and

shoot the visual effects elements in Robert's Austin, Texas-based Troublemaker Studios.

By recording the Sony F-900's HD-SDI signal directly to the hard drive of my Mac G5 via the BlackMagic HD-SDI card, we were able to create elements with easily twice the color space and resolution of HDCAM tape-based acquisition.

Treadmill action composited with Artbeats footage makes a fine ending.

I've used green screen treadmills well over a hundred times and they always add production value. The trick is to match your lighting, angle of view and perspective.

While the white balloon gag can get you close enough for most work, the real tricky bit is in matching the feet to the ground. By having your plates on set and acquiring directly into your computer, you can do a quick test to make sure everything matches before actors are out of costume.

MOTION ENCODING

Motion Encoding might be a little difficult to grasp at first but it represents the future of production. You might as well get a handle on it now.

Systems fire up for another day of production.

The first motion picture to be shot with this methodology was a bold experiment of mythic proportions and involves a lot of characters that you've already met in this book. Big surprise.

The movie is called *Red Riding Hood,* and it is one of those surreptitious little projects that only gets made by sneaking in under the radar. Nearly all of the live action for this movie was shot on blue screen, with real-time, on-set compositing.

The movie was directed by one of the most innovative directors in the business, Randal Kleiser *(Grease, Blue Lagoon, Big Top Pee-Wee, Honey I Blew Up the Kid),* with the gregarious Dave Stump ASC *(X-Men, Blade, Mars Attacks, Stargate),* serving as DP.

Working under Stump, the camera team was charged with operating twin state-of-the-art Thomson Viper cameras. Veteran operators Joe Di Gennaro, Sean Fairburn and your's truly ran this new technology. I know, this seems to be a re-occuring theme.

The action was shot using two Viper cameras that recorded 23.98 progressive images to D5 tape at 4:2:2 in HDStream mode (via the camera's HD-SDI Port). The Vipers were linked to an encoded tracking system that Dave had helped develope and which won him a Technical Achievement Academy Award in 2000.

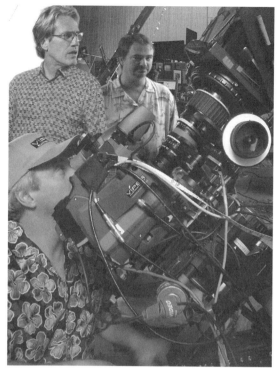

Joe lines up a shot as Randal Kleiser (Left) and Dave Stump look on. If you look closely you can see the eyeball of 1st AC Vince Mata peaking through the gear as he pulls focus.

The data signal from the encoders was then sent to a tracking system developed by Norwegian graphics company Vizrt, which used it to simultaneously drive the 3D sets and environments that were being generated by workstations run by SandMan Studios of Orem, Utah.

Simply put, Motion Encoding uses a system that moves a virtual set in conjunction with the camera. Every move the camera makes is echoed in the virtual set. It is as if the camera were turned into a giant computer mouse that controls the virtual camera in the computer. The set can be entirely CG, SuperFrames or a combinatin of graphic, photographic, video and CG elements.

Aside from the entire production being off the charts technically, was the fact that it was shot almost entirely on bluescreen, with nearly all sets and locations precomped in realtime, live on set.

To accomplish this, an engineering station takes a downconverted feed and, using a conventional switcher, overlays the image with on-set, 3D CG backgrounds, which it pumps back out for viewing reference.

Although this has been done for certain sequences on feature films before, this was the first movie to make such visualization procedures a common practice throughout the entire production.

Dave's take on this whole process was characteristically blasé. *"Since we're encoding data from both cameras on every axis*

Even though the guild frowns upon a DP physically operating a camera, Dave can't help but jump in for a quick spin.

of movement, the actors are free to move naturally without the need to follow a pre-programmed path. It might not sound like such a big thing, but I've shot a lot of movies where the actors were forced to hit an extensive series of marks, and it always seemed to affect their performance. With a musical such as this, I think the added freedom is appreciated by people on both sides of the camera."

Randal Kleiser's view of the process was a bit bolder, *"Obviously, the production environment that we've created here is very advanced. Many of these systems have never worked together or at this resolution, but everything seems to be holding. Now all we need to do is tell a good story."*

With a techno-panorama of more than 30 screens displaying camera image, computer elements, diagnostics, audio and control interfaces, the view at the location becomes a cacophony of components that all contribute to a greater whole. This could easily be the most advanced production metaphor to hit our industry since David Wark Griffith decided it might be nice to move the camera. My wife thinks the process should be called *Geek-O-Rama*.

While everyone else is at lunch, the SandMan crew renders out a few more scenes.

Industry veteran D. Scott Easton *(XXX, The Rookie, Stuart Little, The Lost World: Jurassic Park)*, boldly stepped up to serve as the film's Line Producer. *"This shoot differs from a conventional production in that we're essentially bringing all of the locations to us.*

"There is a great economy with respect to conventional production methodology, but the new technologies have a learning curve that not only includes lots of new equipment and personnel, but an entire new glossary that everyone needs to be familiar with."

Joe Di Gennaro mans the dolly-mounted Viper (Chapman dolly, boom and track, Sachtler fluid head) while Sean and I switch off with the camera that is attached to an AeroHead at the end of a 30ft. AeroCrane.

Both cameras were fitted with a pair of Canon HD 4.7mm to 52mm zooms, the Preston FI+Z MkII three-axis

The author grinds out a shot on the AeroCrane.

wireless lens control system (commonly called Preston FIZ remotes), and multi-axis encoders, which the Vizrt system reads to drive the Softimage-created CG sets in synch with camera output.

Unlike conventional production where the Director cues the DP, who then cues the operator, who rolls and then cues the DP to cue the Director to cue the actors, this process had a few extra elements in it.

There is the CG station that needs to have the image up and "live", the DIT (digital imaging technician) who needs to confirm that all the image and control links are working, the motion tracking group who needs to keep a tight eye on registration and then of course there is the fact that each of these stations introduces a few frames of delay.

Lainie Kazan belts one out. As the camera moves whith her it also drives the camera within the 3D application.

In normal digital production we've learned to deal with delay. A couple frames here or there is nothing to get upset about. This system however had some very big hoops to jump through and by the time the signal finished making its rounds it had nearly three seconds of delay.

Operating a camera at the end of a 30ft crane takes a bit of getting used to when you're looking at a delayed signal. As Sean Fairburn put it, *"You've got three monitors in front of you, all pumping image with different delays, and none of them are in synch with the action that you're covering. Your signal is going out to six different stations that are each tracking, adding, or compositing something to it, and they're all counting on you to nail the shot."*

After tracking several rehearsals while trying to decide which monitor to follow, I glanced at the other stations. The Vizrt guys seemed happy with the tracking data that streamed out of the camera's encoder. The SandMan team, responsible for creating the virtual environment for the shot, seemed happy with the registration to their CGI. Then, I glanced over in Jay Nefcy's direction. He did not look happy.

Nefcy was the show's DIT. He was manning a substantial rack of gear that included, among other things, waveform monitors and the two Panasonic AJ-HD3700AE D5 machines that recorded the 4:2:2 SDI signals out of the Vipers.

Joe Di Gennaro runs through a blocking with Joey Fatone. Note the "garden hose" around his neck.

To create NTSC dailies on set, the cameras had to be genlocked together so that all timecode references (23.8-29.97, etc.) would work in unison. Because the Vipers didn't have "reference out" (a problem that has since been remedied), Stump wired a tri-level synch generator to the multi-pin dongle connection at the back of the cameras. As Di Gennaro put it, *"It's like shooting with a garden hose attached."*

The tri-level sat at the top of a stack of Evertz timecode generators that linked all of the downstream activity, including the compositing switcher, Emile's (our sound designer) audio DAT, and SandMan's CG backgrounds that were being driven by Vizrt's realtime tracking software.

Everything needed the right synch and timecode in order to make Jay happy.

After a quick equipment scan and the flicking of many switches, Jay realized that something had come loose somewhere, and he shifted into a mildly controlled panic. The studio floor looked like free pasta night at the Olive Garden as Jay and I traced and retraced cables that wound off in every direction.

Sean and Randal line up a shot at the AeroHead station.

Joe's camera crew was re-setting for another shot on another stage, so he came over to see how we were doing. I've known Joe for some time now — he has served as DP on a rather extensive list of television shows and motion pictures that I've directed and has as much experience with the Viper as anyone I know. He also has a wry sense of humor that has the unfortunate habit of bubbling to the surface when you need it least, like this particular moment, for instance.

"Randal's on the way over and he's really anxious to shoot," he said, squirting lighter fluid on a raging inferno. *"I sure wouldn't want to keep him waiting."*

Two minutes later, with a simple half-twist of an errant BNC connector, one of a hundred tiny lights blinked on, and Jay settled back with a satisfied look. Disaster averted.

Randal Kleiser pulls up a chair and asks to run through the shot. A few micro adjustments, a quick blocking rehearsal, and three minutes later the shot is in the digital can.

The AeroHead sits at the business end of the 30ft AeroCrane.

While we waited for the crew to make a small adjustment to the lights for our next shot, I shifted into journalistic mode, pulled out my ubiquotious mini-recorder and ask Randal for his take on this unique methodology. "Honey I Blew Up the Kid *was right at the turning point between optical and digital.*

"We did most of the shots optically and a few shots near the end of production digitally because the industry had just started to change over. These days, you'd be hard pressed to even find a house that does opticals."

Dave Stump notices a hot spot and moves the stand-ins a little farther from the wall. I crank the camera back a bit to accommodate, and Randal asks James Jensen, the visual effects producer from SandMan Studios, to put up a different backplate.

Watching the comp monitor, Randal sees a plate he likes and asks for a slight alteration to match the lighting. *"Three minutes,"* Jensen says as Randal sits back down, resuming our conversation.

"So here we are, 10 years later, and we're at another turning point. Unlike the transition to digital, which was mostly about the recording medium, this one is about the basic approach to making movies. We're actually bringing a significant amount of postproduction onto the set and merging it with production. We are redefining the workflow, and I can only see it becoming more integrated as filmmakers realize the creative and financial advantages to working this way. Cutting and pasting the performances of two actors into the same shot, shooting an entire day at magic hour, sets and locations limited only by imagination, not budget: The list goes on and on."

The SandMan crew preps another virtual environment that is built from ArtBeats Library footage.

Almost three minutes to the second, the altered background pops up behind the stand-ins, interrupting our reverie. *"That's it, that's the one I want,"* says Randal. *"Now let's shoot this thing."* Five minutes later, we've got the shot, and the boss is off to the other side of the huge stage to see what Joe's got for him.

Few people have a better vantage point from which to view the binary onslaught than the director's younger brother. Under the watchful eye of the legendary Harrison Ellenshaw, a young Jeff Kleiser painfully crafted digital frames for Disney's 1982 release of *Tron*. Most recently, he served as the senior visual effects supervisor for the latest *X-Men*.

"I'm very excited to see Randal getting into this new technology," Jeff says as we cool off in the breeze of a brand-new, roll-in air conditioner. *"Realtime feedback on-set is so powerful; it's really quite impressive how quickly things are getting lined up and shot."*

Looking across the huge stage, we can see the small crew working away. *"In the 10 minutes that we've been standing here, he's gotten off three shots, two of them were first takes. Randal's a very efficient director, but I don't think that I've ever seen him move so fast with so much confidence."*

We get our hands on a couple of iced Frappuccinos, and between sips Jeff continues promoting the notion that this type of production represents a fundamental change in the moviemaking process.

"We are watching an important change in moviemaking, where we are passing the point of diminishing returns. It's becoming more efficient to make this extra effort in production and reap heavy rewards in post. This methodology should shrink post schedules and budgets significantly."

Echoing that thought is Steve Austin, president of the film's production company, Tag Entertainment. *"We brought this project in for under two million dollars, but the methodology gave us 10 million dollars worth of production value.*

Pretty soon, everyone will be using these technologies to some degree, and the playing field will get leveled once again. For now, and perhaps into the near future, I think

The Vizrt system lines up a CG tree with actor Joey Fatone who is sitting on some blue apple boxes.

that we have a significant edge, one that will give us a distinct advantage in bringing a full catalog to market more cost effectively."

As far as Hollywood motion picture studios go, Tag Entertainment is really quite small. With a little more than 20 titles to its credit *(Black Beauty, The Retrievers, Hansel & Gretel, Miracle Dogs, The Santa Trap)*, the company is unencumbered by the requisite baggage of flashy real estate.

"Technology is the great equalizer," he continues. *"You can make a movie by throwing money at it, or you can make a movie by being smart. Either way, you end up with a movie. Obviously, there are some genres that will be slower to adapt than others. This method of production has so many advantages that even the simplest, contemporary dramas could use it to establish things, such as locations, and develop themes.*

"Want your story to take place in London? Throw up the London plate. Don't like that? Throw up the New York plate. Since all the motion data is there, you can add fog, rain, and atmospheric effects in post. The only limitations are the ones you show up with.

Joey Fatone kicks up some dust as the background is semlessly comped into the truck shot.

"Red Riding Hood *was a great project for this technology because the fairy tale and fantasy worlds give you so much latitude," he continues. "Randal already had an idea about the look he wanted, so we did a few experiments and even printed some tests to film. The results were quite impressive. You can tailor a look to match the story, and I think that's what intrigued Randal about this project.*

"If this was just a normal 35mm movie, I doubt that we would have been able to assemble such a high-caliber crew for this kind of budget. Everyone was so vested in the technology. They wanted to see it work. There were a few glitches here and there, but before you could even build up a good head of worry about it, someone had figured out a solution.

"We made good choices and put a lot of faith in the people we chose. Randal Kleiser, D. Scott Easton, Dave Stump: These are all people that you associate with budgets that have a lot more zeros than ours. They all went above and beyond the call of duty, testing, research- ing, and helping to design this system. The crews they brought to keep the whole show up and running are top-dollar craftsmen."

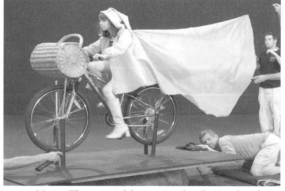

Morgan Thompson pedals up a virtual road to grandmas house.

Thompson, the show's diminutive lead, suddenly rides toward us on her bicycle. Pedals clicking, red cape flapping, she hollers, *"Hi guys. Bye guys,"* and whizzes past. Austin chuckles; *"As you know, there are a lot more regulations with regard to working with children these days. The hours they can work, on-set schooling, and such all has a significant impact on the efficiency of the production, which in turn affects the bottom line. This system is particularly well suited to working with those type of limitations, because you just put them on blue, get their shots, and send 'em home."*

SOFTWARE

Next to religion and politics, there is perhaps no topic that arouses such passion as software. Perhaps it is the fact that the true equity of any software is the time you've invested learning it. No one wants to hear that they've just spent thousands of dollars and years of their life using outdated applications. It all comes down once again to that very basic question: Are you a generalist or a specialist?

With respect to digital moviemaking, do you have an interest in all aspects of production or is there one aspect that you prefer over all others? Do you enjoy learning and working with software or do you see it merely as a tool to help you accomplish your goals? Do you feel better when you are getting a regular paycheck or when you're venturing off on a risky project that you're passionate about?

If this book appeals to you, then you are probably a generalist. My software recommendations are intended for you. There is a very good chance that you'll get your nose bent out of shape if you've invested a lot of time in a piece of software that isn't one of my recommendations. Sorry.

Perhaps you were trying to save money by buying the "off brand." Whatever hardware/software dogma you've bought into will probably still work just fine. It's all just hammers and nails.

You can easily spend tens of thousands of dollars on high-end software applications that will take years to learn, or you can simply hop on Moore's bandwagon and get your hands on some applications that you can start using immediately and are dramatically less expensive.

It is very easy to make complex software. It is very difficult to make powerful software that is easy to use.

At the very top of my list of price/performance, easy-to-use, looks-like-a-million-bucks, must-have software recommendations are Apple's FinalCutPro, Adobe PhotoShop, Adobe After Effects, e-Frontiere's Poser and e-on Software's VUE. If you're a hard-core PC user or you bought the Adobe Production Suite, then feel free to substitute Adobe Premiere for FCP; they are both great applications.

There are lots of other, really great applications out there but these are what I consider to be the essential tools for a contemporary digital movie maker.

Adobe PhotoShop gives you the ability to retouch and build backgrounds and environments and is perhaps the most commonly used software application in motion picture production. It is also the first software application to become integrated into the common vernacular as in, *"I'm going to PhotoShop the fish I caught so it looks bigger."*

Adobe After Effects is easily the most widely used motion graphics application in motion picture production and I would imagine
that it is responsible for more title treatments and visual effects than
every other application combined. The relatively inexpensive, cross-
platform uber-ware is relatively easy to learn and works quite well on
everything from monster workstations to laptops.

Avid once ruled the world of editing, but Apple's FinalCut
was quick to fill the
hole left by Adobe's
withdrawal of
Premiere
from the
Mac.

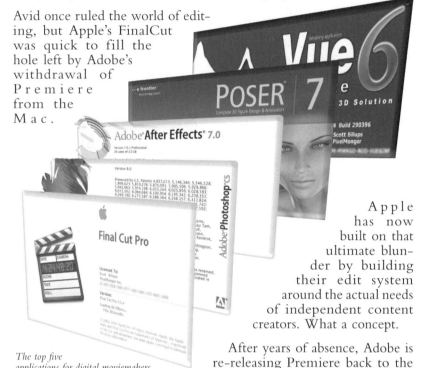

The top five
applications for digital moviemakers.

Apple
has now
built on that
ultimate blun-
der by building
their edit system
around the actual needs
of independent content
creators. What a concept.

After years of absence, Adobe is
re-releasing Premiere back to the
Mac platform but I'm afraid it might
be a matter of too little, too late. Kind of sad really, because Premiere
is a great piece of software and has one of the truly great intervolom-
etrs.

Premiere's cross-platform capabilities make it a top contender in environments that are running both PCs and Macs, and like FCP it runs
quite well on everything from mega-computers to laptops. It also
supports a greater number of color spaces and ingests a wider range of
formats without the guesswork often involved with FCP.

Virtual CG environments were once the providence of mega-shops
like Digital-Domain, ILM and DreamWorks. Their awe-inspiring
images generally only appeared in the mega-budget blockbusters. Not
any more. The single coolest, easiest-to-use and most powerful environmental generator in the motion picture industry is called VUE.

You've seen its images in dozens of huge movies and the really great thing is that this application is fully locked onto Moore's Law. Every version is more powerful, easier-to-use, with faster renders and more realism.

The truly amazing thing to me is that VUE has very French roots. The original name is *Vue d'Esprit* and as the readers of the first or second editions of this book will probably recall, I had quite a few issues with anything French.

Among them were their stubborn adherence to the SECAM video standards, the arrogant approach they took with The CCIR (Comité Consultatif International des Radiocommunications), and the fact that nearly every piece of software they wrote was unforgivably obtuse. I might have even used the term *"frog-ware"* once or twice.

Well, no more. Consider this my official and most humble apology to everything and everyone French.

"Je m'excuse humblement auprès de toute personne française lisant ces mots!"

You will find no disparaging remarks in this or any other book or article I write from now on.

Starting in the $300 range, Vue is a cross-platform powerhouse. It imports character animations and models from many other 3D applications including Poser. Between the two, you could very easily create an entire feature-length motion picture.

In the hands of a master, Vue makes truly spectacular pixel dust.

One of the true maestros of Vue is leading industry matte painter, Chris Stoski. His impressive portfolio includes *Star Wars, Catwoman, The Alamo, The Last Samurai* and *Jurassic Park* to name but a few.

"Before Vue came along, Matte Painters had to rely on photographs, model miniatures or shear painting to create photo-real trees and vegetation. This often presented a problem.

"Relying on photographs can be difficult, you can't always control the camera angle, lighting angle, weather, tree type and the terrain they grow on when you take these photos. These are all variables that stand in the way of the artist's vision.

"An alternative can be to use model miniatures, however, often these tree types look like model-train type of trees that lack all the complexity and weathering that a real forest might have. Lastly, hand-painting the trees is an option, however the drawbacks to this approach is often three-fold, it's very time consuming, it often doesn't look photo-real even when executed by the most experienced hand and finally, 2D hand-painted trees can rarely ever be used in a 3D matte painting where the camera flies through or overtop of the forest canopy.

"Using Vue opens up a whole new world to artists. All of a sudden our hands are untied and using a virtual 3D camera, we can shoot whatever tree type, in any lighting, on any terrain we dream and control multiple variables on both a micro and macro scale. We can even add animation such as leaves blowing in the breeze to create the illusion of life in our matte paintings. This is very difficult if not impossible to do with model miniatures, 2D painted trees or photographs." ~ Chris Stoski

Keep in mind that applications like Maya, SoftImage, and Digital Fusion are fantastically powerful and can do things that are truly amazing.

Even though we use them on a fairly regular basis, their main intent is to facilitate the manufacturing of production elements in an industrialized graphics, factory-type environment.

If that's the kind of thing you want to do for a liv-

Vue's intuitive interface is easy to use, straight from the box.

ing, great; it is not what this book is about. I strongly recommend taking a course, whether on-line or in person at the Gnomon School *(www.thegnomonworkshop.com)*, here in the heart of Hollywood.

Although Poser was mentioned earlier in this chapter, it would be unfair to leave it at that. While it is great at making armies and crowds, it has quite a few other attributes that make it such a great application to have in your tool kit.

Good pre-visualization can shave many hours off of a production schedule and Poser excels at it.

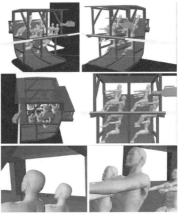

Remember that shot of the rowers from the Replication section of this chapter? We shot that in Lithuania and needed to communicate a very complex set extension/replication gag to a crew that I'd never worked with.

We built a 3D model of the set in an application called Form•Z and then imported the model into Poser where we added the rowers and animated a motion cycle.

Good pre-viz transcends language barriers.

Not only did the Lithuania crew completely understand what I was trying to communicate but they improved on the basic idea with an innovative sliding greenscreen section that allowed us to use only six rowers instead of the original twelve that had been suggested.

I've since shot nearly a dozen shows in Vilnus and always provide them with some solid Poser pre-viz ... which they always improve on.

From ancient warriors to modern leading ladies, every version of POSER lets the camera get a little bit closer. With advanced lip-sync capabilities and motion capture libraries growing daily, the resources for this "killer app" are rapidly approaching a point where we could soon hear a synthetic actor call out "I'm ready for my close-up Mr. DeMille."

PLUG-INS

The digital tsunami that swept over the motion picture industry left in its backwash a business that is fundamentally changed. Every methodology that we've come to embrace has had to adapt not only to a new digital toolset, but to an inherent reinvention of post-production methodology.

When the digital desktop first schmoozed its way into the film industry, it was all about the box. What the computer could do, how dependable and how fast it was. These days, a box is pretty much a box. Whether it has a partially eaten fruit on it or a few emblazoned letters, they all do basically the same things. Like formula race cars, underneath the colorful shells they all run around the same tracks at essentially the same speeds.

The specialized leading edge of digital post-production is now somewhat defined by third party sub-applications called plug-ins.

While not exactly something that could be considered a *"hack,"* plug-ins are greatly expanding the capabilities of software packages by allowing the user to customize and create a growing number of bigger and better looks and effects.

As important as a good computer and a solid suite of master applications are for the digital moviemaker, the true power of contemporary post-production is echoed in the quiver of plug-ins that you use.

Some personal favorites:

Automatic Duck's Pro Import plug-in exports compositions from FinalCutPro and then imports them into After Effects without any codec conversion. It also translates to and from Avid, Premiere and Combustion.

Digital Film Tools was originally developed as the in-house suite of custom applications for an L.A.-based visual effects company. Marco Paolini has brought this rather extensive suite tools to the market in the form of four separate plug-in collections.

55mm is a suite of digital equivalents of conventional glass camera filters, specialized lenses, optical lab processes, film grain, matte generation, exacting color correction as well as natural light and photographic effects.

Digital Film Lab suite is a color timing utility that has created the looks you've seen in numerous big-budget features. The ultimate film look plug-in transforms crisp, harsh-looking video into the softer, more organic look of film using the included 135 preset film looks.

Composite Suite is a group of sophisticated 2D Compositing tools that offers matte manipulation, color correction, grain and lighting effects and eradicates the most common compositing problems.

zMatte is one of the more intelligent blue and green screen keying systems. It is quite easy to use, yet provides the tools you need when presented with a challenging shot, including DV and HD de-artifacting, color suppression, matte manipulation, color correction, edge treatment and light wrapping.

MagicBullet was developed by the good folks at the San Francisco–based Orphanage. Aside from its much touted de-interlacing capabilities, the new Magic Bullet Complete offers a rather extensive workflow solution to post-production.

The basic system starts by exporting your edit from FCP, PremierePro or Avid into the Magic Bullet Colorista, three-way color corrector.

The basic set-up is very similar to industry standards like the Da Vinci, Discrete Lustre, iQ, and other professional grading systems that use the industry standard color model of Lift, Gamma and Gain. The big difference is that this is much easier to use.

Colorista incorporates all the big-time extras such as motion tracking Power Masks and real-time operation. The added bonus it that Colorista uses a 32-bit floating-point plug-in. Stack as many of them on top of each other as you want; you cannot hurt your image.

This is the only affordable plug-in solution that I know of that can time your image without degrading the color space.

After the scene is color corrected, the workflow moves to the Look Suite which offers a quick and easy way to create hundreds of big-budget looks. A new module called InstantHD is perhaps the single best way of up-converting SD footage to HD specs and can be included as part of the work flow.

The Foundry is a four-disk set of plug-ins that represents the single most extensive set of high-end process looks and effects that we use.

The full Tinderbox set contains nearly 50 different filters and each filter is an entire suite of infinitely controllable variations.

A few of the many filter modules include grain tools, sky generators, lightning and electrical effects, blurs, heat haze, droplets, caustics, pattern generators and an extensive suite of distortion filters — and that's just the first disk.

Tinderbox Muzzle Flash, Flow and Fire plug-ins are probably some of the most-used plug-ins in all of visual effects.

I recently shot a motion picture called *LOOK* using Sony F-950 and it came out looking fantastic. Problem was, the entire story was told from the POV of surveillance cameras. It simply looked too good.

The image from the Sony 950 looked so good that we felt guilty degrading it.

We ended up treating the entire movie with a single filter from the Tinderbox Disk 3 collection and were able to come up with over a hundred different looks that really helped sell the concept.

The powerful image processer of the TinderBox "BadTV" module provided enough horsepower to affect the entire motion picture with a wide variety of looks. By batch processing all of the similar shots from each scene in the same filter que, we could set up week-long renders and work on something else while it processed.

RE:Vision Effects makes a couple very useful and much needed tools. ReelSmart Motion Blur adds more natural-looking motion blur to a sequence using single pixel tracking rather than the simple frame-blurring method found in most compositing applications.

Twixtor intelligently slows down, speeds up or changes the frame rate of your image sequences using inter-frame interpolation rather than the simple frame averaging method found in most compositing applications.

Toolfarm.com has an amazing system for finding the right plug-in for your needs. It is called the Plug-in Finder and it has all the plug-ins mentioned here and many more.

The motion graphics side of the Digital Desktop is a subject that is so vast that it would take a very thick book to do it justice. That book is called *Creating Motion Graphics Production* and was written by my good friends Trish and Chris Meyer. *(http://www.cybmotion.com)*

For those just starting out with the computer-based aspects of production or looking to maintain the edge they've already developed, there is no better way to build a solid base of understanding than with the on-line persona of my good friend Lynda Wyman.

Lynda, perhaps more than any other person, is responsible for the vast majority of intelligent software decisions that I've taken credit for throughout my carrier.

Lynda.com is an online training resource that covers nearly every aspect of contemporary digital production.

ABOUT THE AUTHOR

Scott's first paycheck came from veteran ski-movie legend Warren Miller, who paid the sixteen-year-old Billups twenty dollars to ski off a cliff with a camera.

Scott fell in love with film-making and put himself through college with his trusty Arriflex 16ST, shooting for documentary legends such as MacGillivray/Freeman, Wolper Productions and National Geographic. As a junior stringer with WNET he covered Woodstock, at least until the acid kicked in.

After college Scott headed west. Hired by Oscar-winning cinematographer James Wong Howe, Scott continued to work on several of Mr. Howe's commercial accounts after Howe's death, parlaying that into his own ad agency (eighty-five employees in three states). Scott sold his agency and retired in 1983. His retirement lasted a whole four months!

Best known for the hundreds of zany commercials he wrote and directed in the 1980s and '90s, and more recently for the darkly compelling SONY PlayStation commercial that he shot for noted director David Lynch, Scott is widely regarded as one of the preeminent authorities on Digital Cinema production. A popular speaker, Scott is often featured at industry events such as Digital Day at the DGA, the Producers Guild, the Hollywood Post Alliance, and the HD Summit at Universal Studios, and has keynoted NAB, Seybold Seminars, DV Expo and Mac World — twice!

Since the last edition of this book was published, Scott has shot seven motion pictures, five of them digitally. Except for two that were studio projects, all were featured at major festivals like Sundance/Slamdance, Toronto, CineVegas and the HBO Comedy festival in Aspen. All have sold, gone into distribution and made money. In that same time period Scott also worked on more than a dozen award-winning shows for Discovery Channel, History Channel and HBO and contributed to both of this year's non-fiction, prime-time Emmy winners. Scott's collaborations include projects with David Lynch, Mario Van Peebles, Randal Kleiser, Matt Dillon, Spike Lee, Bob Saget, Ice Cube, Chris Rock, Faye Dunaway, Adam Rifkin and Russell Simmons.

As this book goes to press, Scott is directing a twelve-part series for the Discovery Channel as well as a feature for the Universal Studios–based Insomnia Media Group.

You can reach Scott at SB@PixelMonger.com.

FILM DIRECTING: SHOT BY SHOT

VISUALIZING FROM CONCEPT TO SCREEN

STEVEN D. KATZ

BEST SELLER
OVER 190,000 COPIES SOLD!

Film Directing: Shot by Shot — with its famous blue cover — is the best-known book on directing and a favorite of professional directors as an on-set quick reference guide.

This international bestseller is a complete catalog of visual techniques and their stylistic implications, enabling working filmmakers to expand their knowledge.

Contains in-depth information on shot composition, staging sequences, visualization tools, framing and composition techniques, camera movement, blocking tracking shots, script analysis, and much more.

Includes over 750 storyboards and illustrations, with never-before-published storyboards from Steven Spielberg's *Empire of the Sun*, Orson Welles' *Citizen Kane*, and Alfred Hitchcock's *The Birds*.

"(To become a director) you have to teach yourself what makes movies good and what makes them bad. John Singleton has been my mentor... he's the one who told me what movies to watch and to read Shot by Shot.*"*
> – Ice Cube, *New York Times*

"A generous number of photos and superb illustrations accompany each concept, many of the graphics being from Katz' own pen... Film Directing: Shot by Shot *is a feast for the eyes."*
> – *Videomaker* Magazine

"... demonstrates the visual techniques of filmmaking by defining the process whereby the director converts storyboards into photographed scenes."
> – *Back Stage Shoot*

"Contains an encyclopedic wealth of information."
> – *Millimeter* Magazine

STEVEN D. KATZ is also the author of *Film Directing: Cinematic Motion*.

$27.95 · 366 PAGES · ORDER NUMBER 7RLS · ISBN: 0-941188-10-8

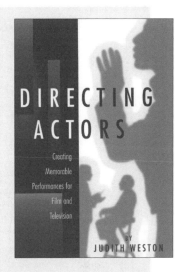

THE WRITER'S JOURNEY
3RD EDITION

MYTHIC STRUCTURE FOR WRITERS

CHRISTOPHER VOGLER

BEST SELLER
OVER 170,000 COPIES SOLD!

See why this book has become an international best seller and a true classic. *The Writer's Journey* explores the powerful relationship between mythology and storytelling in a clear, concise style that's made it required reading for movie executives, screenwriters, playwrights, scholars, and fans of pop culture all over the world.

Both fiction and nonfiction writers will discover a set of useful myth-inspired storytelling paradigms (i.e., "The Hero's Journey") and step-by-step guidelines to plot and character development. Based on the work of Joseph Campbell, *The Writer's Journey* is a must for all writers interested in further developing their craft.

The updated and revised third edition provides new insights and observations from Vogler's ongoing work on mythology's influence on stories, movies, and man himself.

"This book is like having the smartest person in the story meeting come home with you and whisper what to do in your ear as you write a screenplay. Insight for insight, step for step, Chris Vogler takes us through the process of connecting theme to story and making a script come alive."
> – Lynda Obst, Producer, *Sleepless in Seattle, How to Lose a Guy in 10 Days;*
> Author, *Hello, He Lied*

"This is a book about the stories we write, and perhaps more importantly, the stories we live. It is the most influential work I have yet encountered on the art, nature, and the very purpose of storytelling."
> – Bruce Joel Rubin, Screenwriter, *Stuart Little 2, Deep Impact,*
> *Ghost, Jacob's Ladder*

CHRISTOPHER VOGLER is a veteran story consultant for major Hollywood film companies and a respected teacher of filmmakers and writers around the globe. He has influenced the stories of movies from *The Lion King* to *Fight Club* to *The Thin Red Line* and most recently wrote the first installment of *Ravenskull*, a Japanese-style manga or graphic novel. He is the executive producer of the feature film *P.S. Your Cat is Dead* and writer of the animated feature *Jester Till*.

$26.95 · 300 PAGES · ORDER NUMBER 76RLS · ISBN: 193290736x

FILM & VIDEO BOOKS

Archetypes for Writers: Using the Power of Your Subconscious
Jennifer Van Bergen / $22.95

Art of Film Funding, The: Alternate Financing Concepts
Carole lee Dean / $26.95

Cinematic Storytelling: The 100 Most Powerful Film Conventions Every
Filmmaker Must Know / Jennifer Van Sijll / $24.95

Complete Independent Movie Marketing Handbook, The: Promote, Distribute
& Sell Your Film or Video / Mark Steven Bosko / $39.95

Creating Characters: Let Them Whisper Their Secrets
Marisa D'Vari / $26.95

Crime Writer's Reference Guide, The: 1001 Tips for Writing the Perfect Crime
Martin Roth / $20.95

Cut by Cut: Editing Your Film or Video
Gael Chandler / $35.95

Digital Filmmaking 101, 2nd Edition: An Essential Guide to Producing
Low-Budget Movies / Dale Newton and John Gaspard / $26.95

Directing Actors: Creating Memorable Performances for Film and Television
Judith Weston / $26.95

Directing Feature Films: The Creative Collaboration Between Directors,
Writers, and Actors / Mark Travis / $26.95

Elephant Bucks: An Insider's Guide to Writing for TV Sitcoms
Sheldon Bull / $24.95

Eye is Quicker, The: Film Editing; Making a Good Film Better
Richard D. Pepperman / $27.95

Fast, Cheap & Under Control: Lessons Learned from the Greatest Low-Budget
Movies of All Time / John Gaspard / $26.95

Fast, Cheap & Written That Way: Top Screenwriters on Writing for Low-Budget
Movies / John Gaspard / $26.95

Film & Video Budgets, 4th Updated Edition
Deke Simon and Michael Wiese / $26.95

Film Directing: Cinematic Motion, 2nd Edition
Steven D. Katz / $27.95

Film Directing: Shot by Shot, Visualizing from Concept to Screen
Steven D. Katz / $27.95

Film Director's Intuition, The: Script Analysis and Rehearsal Techniques
Judith Weston / $26.95

Film Production Management 101: The Ultimate Guide for Film and Television
Production Management and Coordination / Deborah S. Patz / $39.95

Filmmaking for Teens: Pulling Off Your Shorts
Troy Lanier and Clay Nichols / $18.95

First Time Director: How to Make Your Breakthrough Movie
Gil Bettman / $27.95

From Word to Image: Storyboarding and the Filmmaking Process
Marcie Begleiter / $26.95

Hollywood Standard, The: The Complete and Authoritative Guide to Script
Format and Style / Christopher Riley / $18.95

Independent Film Distribution: How to Make a Successful End Run Around
the Big Guys / Phil Hall / $26.95

Independent Film and Videomakers Guide – 2nd Edition, The: Expanded and
Updated / Michael Wiese / $29.95

Inner Drives: How to Write and Create Characters Using the Eight Classic
Centers of Motivation / Pamela Jaye Smith / $26.95

I'll Be in My Trailer!: The Creative Wars Between Directors & Actors
John Badham and Craig Modderno / $26.95

Moral Premise, The: Harnessing Virtue & Vice for Box Office Success
Stanley D. Williams, Ph.D. / $24.95

Myth and the Movies: Discovering the Mythic Structure of 50 Unforgettable
Films / Stuart Voytilla / $26.95

On the Edge of a Dream: Magic and Madness in Bali
Michael Wiese / $16.95

Perfect Pitch, The: How to Sell Yourself and Your Movie Idea to Hollywood
Ken Rotcop / $16.95

Power of Film, The:
Howard Suber / $27.95

Psychology for Screenwriters: Building Conflict in your Script
William Indick, Ph.D. / $26.95

Save the Cat!: The Last Book on Screenwriting You'll Ever Need
Blake Snyder / $19.95

Save the Cat! Goes to the Movies: The Screenwriter's Guide to Every Story
Ever Told / Blake Snyder / $24.95

Screenwriting 101: The Essential Craft of Feature Film Writing
Neill D. Hicks / $16.95

Screenwriting for Teens: The 100 Principles of Screenwriting Every Budding
Writer Must Know / Christina Hamlett / $18.95

Script-Selling Game, The: A Hollywood Insider's Look at Getting Your Script
Sold and Produced / Kathie Fong Yoneda / $16.95

Selling Your Story in 60 Seconds: The Guaranteed Way to get Your Screenplay
or Novel Read / Michael Hauge / $12.95

Setting Up Your Scenes: The Inner Workings of Great Films
Richard D. Pepperman / $24.95

Setting Up Your Shots: Great Camera Moves Every Filmmaker Should Know
Jeremy Vineyard / $19.95

Shaking the Money Tree, 2nd Edition: The Art of Getting Grants and
Donations for Film and Video Projects / Morrie Warshawski / $26.95

Sound Design: The Expressive Power of Music, Voice, and Sound Effects in
Cinema / David Sonnenschein / $19.95

Special Effects: How to Create a Hollywood Film Look on a Home Studio
Budget / Michael Slone / $31.95

Stealing Fire From the Gods, 2nd Edition: The Complete Guide to Story for
Writers & Filmmakers / James Bonnet / $26.95

Ultimate Filmmaker's Guide to Short Films, The: Making It Big in Shorts
Kim Adelman / $16.95

Way of Story, The: The Craft & Soul of Writing
Catherine Anne Jones / $22.95

Working Director, The: How to Arrive, Thrive & Survive in the Director's Chair
Charles Wilkinson / $22.95

Writer's Journey, – 3rd Edition, The: Mythic Structure for Writers
Christopher Vogler / $26.95

Writing the Action Adventure: The Moment of Truth
Neill D. Hicks / $14.95

Writing the Comedy Film: Make 'Em Laugh
Stuart Voytilla and Scott Petri / $14.95

Writing the Killer Treatment: Selling Your Story Without a Script
Michael Halperin / $14.95

Writing the Second Act: Building Conflict and Tension in Your Film Script
Michael Halperin / $19.95

Writing the Thriller Film: The Terror Within
Neill D. Hicks / $14.95

Writing the TV Drama Series – 2nd Edition: How to Succeed as a
Professional Writer in TV / Pamela Douglas / $26.95

DVD & VIDEOS

Field of Fish: VHS Video
Directed by Steve Tanner and Michael Wiese, Written by Annamaria Murphy / $9.95

Hardware Wars: DVD / Written and Directed by Ernie Fosselius / $14.95

Sacred Sites of the Dalai Lamas – DVD, The: A Pilgrimage to Oracle Lake
A Documentary by Michael Wiese / $24.95